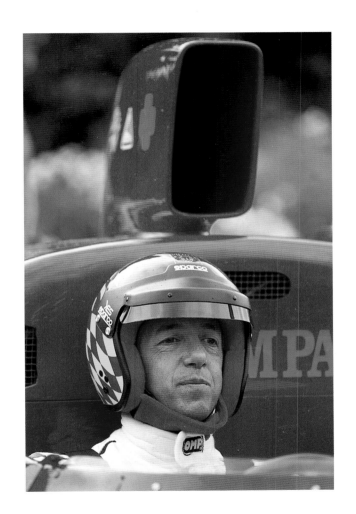

How to Photograph Cars

James Mann

MBI Publishing Company

First published in 2002 by MBI Publishing Company, Galtier Plaza, Suite 200, 380 Jackson Street, St. Paul, MN 55101-3885 USA

MBI Publishing Company books are also available at discounts in bulk quantity for industrial or sales-promotional use. For details write to Special Sales Manager at Motorbooks International Wholesalers & Distributors, Galtier Plaza, Suite 200, 380 Jackson Street, St. Paul, MN 55101-3885 USA

Library of Congress Cataloging-in-Publication Data Available

ISBN 0-7603-1243-5

Acquisitions Editor: Lee Klancher
Project Editor: Kris Palmer
Designer: Chris Fayers
Printed in China

To Sarah

Acknowledgments

With many thanks to the following people for their help and encouragement during the making of this book: Sarah Picot, Jonathon Topps, Steve J. Benbow, Zack Miller, Tim Parker, Lee Klancher, Mark Hughes, Luke Parminter, John Colley

I also used a number of other people's books for reference for which I am grateful.
Speed by E. S. Tompkins
Basic Photography by M. J. Langford
A Practical Guide to Creative Photography by Kodak
Introductory Photography Course by John Hedgecoe
Jacques-Henri Lartigue by Thames and Hudson

All the photographs in this book were taken by the author using a Canon EOS 1, EOS 5, and D60.

Cover and title pictures:

On the front cover: This Porsche was shot using one of the author's custom camera mounts that places the camera outside of the car. *James Mann*

On the frontispiece: Portraits don't have to be posed; they can be candid. This is much easier with a long lens because the subject may not even notice you're taking a picture and won't react self-consciously. 200mm 1/125th f4.5. *James Mann*

On the title page: Editing your pictures will teach you how to recognize a good image when you see one. The Mille Miglia-winning 1955 Mercedes 300SLR and its original team of Stirling Moss and Denis Jenkinson in the cockpit at the end of the first straight at the Goodwood Festival of Speed. 200mm f4.5 500th sec. *James Mann*

Contents: Shooting against the light is a good option when the sun is low in the sky. Be careful to shield the lens itself from flare. 180mm f5.6 1/125th sec. *James Mann*

On the back cover: This is viewed from inside the cove looking back toward the camera, which is set up for a profile shot. The boards flag any direct light from hitting the car and provide the darkness behind the camera to avoid any reflection into the side.

Contents

Foreword

My career in photography spans almost 50 years and many of these years have been spent trackside with my camera at racetracks everywhere. It is a pleasure to write an introduction to James Mann's new book *How To Photograph Cars*. Between the two of us perhaps we can pass on a few tips to the many aspiring photographers out there.

Not only have I done straight-race photography, but I have been active in the commercial car world as well; for example, doing work for Audi North America on their TT sports car introduction and on the R8 race car in the American Le Mans Series. On this project I worked with my designer closely on selection of images and layout—on the TT project the different locations for the shoot were all important and we worked hard to find sites that would be ideal for the new Audi. Recalling these projects I can say that good preparation was paramount. We brainstormed for hours on the many possibilities that were available—we chose an ice rink, a blacksmith shop, and a typical California barn as some of the locations. This project and the R8 portfolio of images were dream commissions.

Recalling the Audi commission and my race photography, I am able to sum up what it takes to succeed in this very competitive line of work. First and foremost, your enthusiasm will in the end carry the day. You do not need the very latest in equipment (I recently made some wonderful images with a $10 child's camera from China called DIANA). If you have a visual gift, as well as a passion for photography and cars, you are bound to be successful. Have your camera with you everywhere and throw away the lens cap.

—Jesse Alexander

Introduction

This sort of spectacular shot can only be set up with the help of the fire department. 300mm f5.6 1/500 second.

This book came about as I remembered the struggles I had as a new staff photographer on a car magazine. I was trying to learn all the techniques necessary to do the job and had no one to ask.

This may seem strange, for I was part of a large photographic department and many of the other "snappers" were car guys. There was then, and there still exists today, a certain secrecy and myth about how these photo wizards worked their magic and pulled marvelous pictures out of the hat.

All the photographic manuals I looked at, and what I learned at art college, told me very little about shooting cars and went into so much detail about how the camera works and the physics of light; I found it very difficult to extract anything useful in practice.

Photography, like any art, is a way of seeing things differently. It requires training your eye to see selectively as the viewfinder does and, like the other arts of painting or drawing, it can be taught. You don't need the latest Nikon Digital SLR to turn out great photos; some of the world's best photographers use completely manual cameras and the most basic materials to give them much more control over the final image.

In the following pages I intend to let you in on many techniques that will, with a bit of practice, have you shooting like a professional and increase your "hit" rate immediately. Whether you are shooting for your club magazine, at the races for competitors, or just for fun, I hope that the techniques in this book, coupled with your own ideas, will help you to get as much out of photographing cars as I do.

Damon Hill behind the wheel of a Ferrari 250GTO. Choosing the right spot at the racetrack is one of the key elements to shooting great racing images. 200mm f4.5 1/640 second.

Left: Fantastic locations make fantastic photographs. Take a compass when you are location hunting to show where the sun will set. 180mm f32 8 seconds. **Below:** The appearance of speed is deceptive. This Lotus Elise is being pushed by the photographer at around 1 mile per hour. 20-35mm f16 2 seconds.

Shooting a car in an infinity cove offers a wholly artificial world where the photographer has total control over the environment. This is a 1969 Renault Alpine being prepared for the salon treatment.

Chapter 1
Equipment

With practice and care, you can achieve good results on basic cameras.

Some of the my favorite action images were taken by a French photographer named Jacques-Henri Lartigue, who turned out his best photographs while under the age of 18 by using a very basic focal plane camera at the beginning of the twentieth century. He photographed his friends in their soapboxes and passing cars and came up with remarkable results.

So with the simplest of cameras, you can get great images. You don't have to have the latest automatic digital SLR.

35MM AND APS COMPACT CAMERAS

By far the most common camera around today is the compact camera. They are great for people pictures and you can shoot cars with them too.

Even though many have zoom lenses, the sharpest have fixed lenses. Long zooms are difficult to hold steady on a compact camera and their lens quality can be compromised by the tiny size they have to fit into.

Never crop too tight on a subject when shooting with a compact camera. You won't get exactly what you see through the viewfinder, due to it being offset to one side or above. It's very easy to think you just captured the greatest shot only to find that you've chopped one end off the frame.

Most of these cameras have automatic exposure with a flash, but as your skills and photographic imagination expand, you may not want the camera to decide for you

Compact cameras are great for getting candid pictures close up but not ideal if you want to shoot action at the racetrack.

Digital cameras have a screen on the back that will show you whether you got the shot. Trashing your mistakes allows you more images on your flash card.

the amount of light you need. For this reason, select a camera that allows you to turn the flash off or adjust its power.

Look for a tripod fixing on the base. Tripods are useful for timed exposures where you want to be in the picture, or for shooting at night. In the latter case, where you'll use a slow shutter speed, a tripod will hold the camera steadier than can be done by hand.

A wrist strap is the most useful way to carry a compact and it's not bulky, so you can put it in your pocket for convenient storage.

DIGITAL COMPACT

Many of the techniques that apply to the film compact camera also apply to the digital compact. This is because, at their simplest, both types of cameras are fully automatic and take over exposure control. They often have a number of preprogrammed settings for a variety of scenes as well.

The preprogrammed settings usually do not include fast action so you will need to experiment with your camera to learn the best setting. Landscape is likely to be the most useful program, but you might also use portrait or the close-up option for details. Digital cameras are excellent at working in much lower light conditions than film so you can try some night or evening shots. You may be able to adjust the effective film speed or ASA to increase the sensitivity; however, this is not an option on the more basic models and any work to lighten the image will have to be done later on the computer.

It's a good idea to use a tripod or monopod when using any long lens to reduce camera shake. This is particularly a good idea with the digital compact because the body of the camera is so small that it is difficult to hold it still.

After you have downloaded your image from your digital camera to your computer, the sky's the limit on what you can do to play around with it. This is hiked up on contrast by 80 percent, brightened 20 percent with cyan added 10 percent, all of which you'll find on the image menu.

With a 35mm SLR camera you can crop your image exactly as you want it in the viewfinder. 300mm f5.6 1/125 second.

Take a few images on different programs and review them on the LCD screen on the back or download them to check out what works best. Delete the failures but keep an open mind; as sometimes the most creative images come out of the most unlikely situations.

35mm SLR

The great advantage of a single lens reflex (SLR) camera is the accuracy with which it captures your desired photograph. Due to a system of prisms and mirrors, when you look through an SLR's viewfinder, you are actually looking through the camera's lens: what you see is what you get. This allows you to compose and expose your image accurately using the through-the-lens (TTL) metering system, which all SLRs now have.

You can also change lenses simply and quickly, allowing you to get very different shots from similar positions. Useful lenses vary from about 20mm to 300mm. Although some track photographers will have lenses of 600mm and longer, they are very expensive. Mirror lenses are much lighter and cheaper than their telephoto alternatives but can suffer a bit on quality and may have a fixed aperture. Likewise, there are fish-eye lenses down to 6mm, but these are highly specialized and are rarely used in the magazines.

Many photographers now use zoom lenses, which have improved enormously over the last ten years. It's best to go for two or three lenses rather than one zoom that takes in the whole 20-300mm range because they can be compromised on quality, especially at the limits of their use. A 20-35mm lens is very useful for close-up action, where you might be panning a car from the inside of a corner, and 80-200mm is a good portrait and fast-action lens-it won't distort the image and it keeps the photographer a safe distance away from the action.

If you can afford it, a fixed 300mm and a 50mm macro lens should make up the rest of your equipment as they will allow you to shoot dramatic cornering and close-ups, but they're not essential for what I will show you in this book.

Although most professional cameras can be used fully automated, many photographers prefer to shoot manually to retain control on the whole process. Canon EOS 1 and Nikon F3.

Autofocus or Manual

Most lenses made today are autofocus with a switch to go to manual. Despite the occasional convenience of the autofocus feature, many photographers prefer to focus manually if there's time. Autofocus can be fooled by reflections and moving objects. Also, the object you wish to put in focus may not be the one the lens is most directly pointed at. Like old-school photographers, you may come to prefer manual focus, and only switch to auto for that occasional grabbed image.

Keep in mind that the lens must be matched properly to the camera or it will not work. If you shop for the lens individually, confirm its compatibility with your camera before you buy.

Auto Exposure

Automatic exposure operates from an average light meter reading taken through the lens. As with autofocus, you may want the option to overrule it and vary your exposures according to the subject. By using this option and a manual light meter, you may avoid wasting many rolls of film and your valuable time and effort.

You can take two separate readings with a manual meter. You can measure the light falling on the subject, or the light reflected back from it. In cloudy conditions you can let the camera do the work and rely on your built-in meter, but if it's sunny you may need a hand-held exposure meter to get a really accurate reading. Try to get one that will balance flash and daylight to help in low and tricky light conditions.

Auto exposure can be switched to manual using a function on the camera body, whereas autofocus is usually turned on and off on the lens itself. Different SLR cameras will have a variety of metering patterns that the user can switch between depending on the subject. This could be center weighted, spot, or a general exposure taken from a number of points around the viewfinder.

The meter will measure the light coming through the lens, and in automatic mode it will set the camera shutter speed and aperture for you. Shutter speeds and apertures govern how much light the film is exposed to. If you switch to manual exposure the camera will tell you using either a LCD display or a needle whether you need to adjust the aperture or shutter speed yourself. This is important because many action photos need a specific shutter speed to work properly and you can't rely on the camera to get it right.

The aperture is mounted inside the lens. Using an iris capable of contracting and dilating like your eye's own, it varies the amount of light going through it. More specifically, it varies the frequency of the light waves that pass through. The aperture's settings are measured using a scale known as f-stops. Each f-stop is equal to the focal length of the lens, divided by the diameter of the aperture opening in millimeters. Thus, a 50mm lens paired with a 12.5mm aperture opening would have an f-stop of 4. Since the aperture measurement is the fraction's denominator, as the f-stop number goes up, the aperture opening goes down. Each consecutive f-stop setting halves the amount of light permitted through the lens, starting with a large aperture of f1.4, and decreasing by one-half each time down to a small aperture of f32. Most lenses today have a usable aperture range from f2.8 or f4 to f22.

Aperture settings affect a photograph's depth of field, which describes what range of depth in the photograph is in focus. Higher f-stop settings, and their corresponding small aperture openings, produce clarity of focus at a broader depth. With low f-stop settings, and therefore large aperture openings, the primary subject of the photograph

will be in focus, but objects will become less distinct as they get nearer or farther away from the primary subject. Depth of field is a valuable tool, allowing the photographer to direct the viewer's attention to particular areas of the photograph by controlling how much of it is in focus. Using differing apertures also allows you to exaggerate or suppress the appearance of depth in the photo.

Be experimental with your digital camera—you've got nothing to lose. If you don't like the image just delete it and try something else. This is shot handheld in low light at 1/4 second with 80-200mm zoomed in during the exposure.

DIGITAL SLR

A digital SLR works in exactly the same way as a normal SLR, but instead of recording the image on actual film, it records it on a reusable compact flash card or mini-hard drive. These cards vary in memory capacity, allowing many combinations of mage sizes, depending on the quality required.

A digital SLR allows you to see the images on an LCD screen both before and immediately after you've taken them. This allows you to edit as you go, so only your favorite pictures are saved and space is conserved on the memory card.

INSTANT FILM CAMERAS

There are quite a few makes of instant film cameras around but they are not ideal for shooting cars. They tend to be bulky and have a fixed lens, and with the arrival of digital compact cameras where you can preview the image, they leave a lot to be desired. Instant cameras are cheap but the film is not. Their best use is probably for shooting people with their cars.

Even though the compact flash card is quite expensive, you only need one and it frees you from film's developing and printing costs. You can make a print of a digital image, but you don't need to. They can be stored on your computer, saved to CD-ROM, and transmitted like any other piece of digital information.

FLASH GUNS

Flash guns have come a long way in the last ten years. Most built-in flashes in a compact camera are totally automatic and work with the exposure meter to light the subject accurately. The golden rule here is that a compact camera flash is not very powerful and the furthest it will go is about fifteen feet, working best at about six feet. This does vary a little with a faster film or a digital camera, but don't bother wasting your time at Le Mans.

Some 35mm SLRs have a built-in flash that is equally puny in the face of a far subject at night. The best way to get results from these types of flash guns is to use them in fill-in mode. In low light or against the sky they can be very effective on slow shutter speeds to fill in the foreground or partially freeze the action. They are also good at an indoor car show where there are lots of differing light sources and an ambient exposure would produce weird colors on the subject.

Most SLRs have a separate flash gun that attaches to the top of the camera at a hotshoe. Simple cameras will have a manual flash that you have to set yourself, judging the distance to the subject and adjusting the aperture to match a table on the back of the gun.

More sophisticated cameras have a dedicated system where the flash gun measures the amount of light and works with the camera to expose the subject correctly for you. As with any automatic exposure meter, it can be fooled by reflections or shiny surfaces, so you need to watch out for these and compensate. If you are lighting a particularly light or dark subject, bracket your exposures to be sure of getting it right. Beware of shooting with a reflective surface like a mirror or a window directly behind your subject. If you can't avoid it, move to the side so that any light bounces away from the camera.

Small camera-top flashes will go up to forty feet at full power but this quickly drains the batteries. Larger battery packs are available that you can clip onto your belt and this is a good compromise for moving up to the bigger flash guns that clamp to the bottom of the camera.

TRIPODS

A good tripod is an essential piece of equipment. Tripods come in all sizes–from the miniatures designed for compacts that will fit in your pocket to monsters you can barely lift. You will need one that is light and easy to adjust so you can set it up quickly and won't worry about carrying it around all day. Good models come in two parts, the legs and the head. Go for a metal one that comes to about knee-high when collapsed and to eye level when extended. The head should have three planes of adjustment with locking handles or catches and either a screw fit or a quick-release mounting plate for the camera.

When you look at a new tripod, perform a simple test to ensure it meets your needs. Attach your biggest lens to your camera and mount it to the tripod at the highest extension to see if there is any wobble.

The alternative to a tripod is a monopod. This consists of a telescopic pole with a very simple screw fit on the top. It is often used by racetrack photographers to support their long lenses. It's much lighter and smaller to carry but is no good at all when the light really goes and you have to slow down your shutter speed. Since the photographer has to hold the camera body still, your pictures can easily suffer from camera shake.

CAMERA BAGS

There are hundreds of shapes and sizes of camera bags on the market today but as the amount of gear you have to carry around gets heavier and heavier, the backpack set-up is hard to beat. Look for a bag with two or three major compartments and a similar number of side pockets. It should have padded dividers and a reinforced base. The straps should be wide, padded, and adjustable, and on a backpack there should be a waist-belt. The different pockets should have zips or strong fasteners to close them. Good bags will have a special film compartment as well. Some camera bags are waterproof or made of a material that can be sprayed with a waterproofing protectant. With all the expensive equipment in your bag, you'll want to keep water out.

Many professional photographers suffer from bad backs due to hulking around a camera bag on one shoulder. Although a backpack is not quite as accessible, it may save you a trip to the chiropractor.

HIRING EQUIPMENT

You don't have to own all the camera gear you need—you can hire it. This is particularly useful for specialist gadgets, such as wireless triggers or long and expensive lenses. A 400mm f2.8 lens costs over $10,000 to buy, but only about $80 a day to hire. you will be required to put down the full value of the equipment as a security deposit, so make sure your credit cards are in full working order. You'll find hire departments, or rental equipment, at most professional camera shops.

CAMERA CARE

There are two things that are bad news for the delicate components that make up your camera gear: being dropped and getting wet. A good camera bag can help out in both these situations. If it's well padded and waterproofed you should be able to avoid expensive repairs. However sometimes your camera gear might get wet and if it does it might even stop working due to electrical connections failure.

If you suspect that it might rain and you're going to be out in it, carry a chamois leather big enough to cover the camera and lens. This will soak up a lot of water and you can also use it to wipe the lens. As soon as you can, dry off the outside of the camera with a soft cloth, remove the lens, open the back, and place it in a warm, dry room. Put the lenses (without their end caps) and anything else that got wet in there too, and in a few hours it should be back to normal.

This approach usually works for thunderstorms or a very quick dip in the river, but anything longer or involving salt water is more serious. Get your camera to the nearest repair shop immediately because it may have to dismantled completely. Don't try to do it yourself. If you ever have to store your gear, get a few small bags of silica gel from a friendly camera store and pop them in Ziploc bags with the body and lenses to keep out any moisture.

Dropped camera gear may also require a trip to the repair shop but it's a lot more rugged than it used to be. I've seen equipment hit by race cars, dropped out of a balloon, and even run over get up and finish the day's work. A good idea for all SLR lenses is to fit them with a skylight or an ultraviolet filter. This will protect the outer surface of the lens and does very little to alter your pictures. Fitting a lens hood will also give some protection as well as saving your pictures from flare, if you happen to shoot too close to the light.

Extremes of Heat and cold should also be avoided if you want your equipment to remain in tip-top condition. Temperature over 45°C/120°F and below −10°C/−15°F cause most electronics start to play up. If you have to shoot in these conditions and experience problems, keep the camera cool or warm in a vehicle and only shoot in short bursts of a few minutes at a time.

You may suffer from a fogging inside the lens if the difference between inside and outside temperatures and humidity is too much, so try to regulate how much you warm up or cool down the camera to a minimum. If you do get fogging you'll just have to wait a few minutes for it to clear. In the cold, remove the batteries and put them in a warm pocket while you are waiting to shoot and they will perform much better.

Last, but not least, there's good old dust and dirt. You should try to avoid situations where you get your gear dirty, but it's not always possible out in the field. You can wipe off any dirt on the body with a soft, damp cloth. Lenses and the viewfinder should only be cleaned with a special lens cloth but in an emergency I tend to use a cotton T-shirt. You should never touch the mirror in an SLR camera because it's very delicately balanced and easily scratched. If you have to clean it, do so carefully with a fine paintbrush.

REVIEW

- **Large aperture or small f-stop number = small depth of field.**
- **Small aperture or big f-stop number = large depth of field.**
- **Use your tripod.**
- **Choose a camera with both manual and auto settings.**
- **Look after your equipment.**
- **Buy a good camera bag.**

To check sharpness on your negatives and transparencies it's a good idea to buy a good photographic magnifier or loop. You can hold your film up to a shaded window or look at it on a lightbox.

FILM CHOICES

Or should that read film or electronic media choices? For as technology advances, prices continue to drop for digital cameras. Whereas only the wealthy pro used digital a few years ago, it's now well on the way to taking over film.

There's more to it than just color or black and white. You'll need to think about what you are going to do with the pictures that you produce.

The finished size of the images will determine which film you choose. Whether the subject is moving and how bright a day it is will also have an impact on what film to use. You can avoid many disappointments by choosing the right film at the start. Although there are hundreds of different types and makes, most of these are for highly specialized uses. There are only a few that you will probably end up using regularly.

These wheel rims were shot on Agfa Scala black-and-white transparency film at the factory. Specialist films like this are interesting options but can only be processed at certain photographic labs.

EQUIPMENT LIST

APS/35mm or digital compact camera

SLR camera capable of manual and auto operation

20-35mm zoom

50mm macro

70-200mm zoom

Skylight/UV filters

300mm

Camera bag

Flash gun with both manual and auto functions

Light meter

Tripod

Transparency and Print Film

Print film has been around as long as photography has—more than 150 years—but since the war it has become the poor relation to transparency in the professional field.

Print film uses a negative process that is turned into a positive when it is printed; this is a simple, fairly foolproof system. It has a broad exposure latitude, which means that it doesn't matter if you don't have ideal light conditions or have to grab a picture without the benefit of time or lengthy preparation. It also is quite cheap and so easy to print, particularly black and white, that a smart six-year-old could do it with modern chemicals and procedures.

If you want to adjust the image after you've got a print, you can scan it into your computer using a simple flat-bed scanner and then manipulate the picture using one of the myriad photo retouching packages available.

Transparency film uses a positive process that is complicated and can be expensive to print. Its main advantage is that a well-taken transparency will always be sharper than a print for reproduction in magazines or books, because it is the first generation and not a second generation print as with the negative film.

This film is limited in other ways as well. It has a very narrow usable exposure latitude and it's vital that you meter carefully when using transparency film or detail could easily be lost in the shadows or the highlights.

Transparency film suffers from a narrow latitude for color temperature. It works well in daylight but if you want to shoot indoors or with artificial lighting, a special tungsten film is needed or color correction filters must be used.

Transparency film is also not very easy to process and print yourself and if you want to scan it you'll need a transparency hood for your flatbed or a special scanner designed to take it.

Despite all these potential problems, it is still first choice for many professional photographers due to its superior quality over the other available media. Some of these devotees may be switching over to print film, which has improved by leaps and bounds with faster speeds and finer grain. With better digital printing techniques, it is nearing the quality of transparency film.

ASA/DIN

This is the actual speed of the film—how sensitive it is for light. It is one of the most important choices you'll make when buying your film, because it may determine the quality of the final image and what you can do with it.

Low speeds such as ASA 25 to 100 are finer grain and sharper and are suitable for brightly lit subjects or if you are going to blow the image up to a large size, say over 16x12 inches. These are also low contrast, i.e., they will give an excellent range of colors and tones all the way from black (shadow) to white (highlight). Because they have a low sensitivity to light, shutter speeds may be low and you may need a tripod.

Mid-range films such as ASA 200 or 400 are more popular because they allow a faster shutter speed with less chance of camera shake and can be used in lower light, but they are grainier. Blow-ups are okay to around 10x 8 inches. These are medium contrast with a good range of tones and colors.

Fast and push process films are becoming much more popular and are available at most camera stores. They range from ASA 800 to 3200, but actually you can push them past ASA 50,000.

Shot to look like old film, this is Fuji ASA 800 print film cross-processed through transparency chemicals. A similar effect can be achieved by desaturating the image in a photo retouching package on your computer.

In difficult light situations you can push film up to two stops without much loss of quality, but you must adjust the whole roll, mark it carefully, and tell your processor. ASA 100 rated at ASA 80 and pushed two stops to ASA 320 to achieve 1/500 second at f2.8.

They can be used in low or very low light situations and can be seriously grainy. At the moment only print film offers this adaptability. These are high or very high contrast and consequently tend to have a limited range of tones and problems with color saturation at the very high speeds (over ASA 3000).

Digital media can deal with most light levels with the advantage that you can switch between effective ASA from one image to the next. Digital also deals very well with a variety of light sources from daylight to neon or tungsten without any color correction needed. The number of images you want on the "film" also determines the quality, because the file has a finite size. So you can have a small number of large, high-quality images or lots of small, low-resolution images.

Once saved, the pictures can be either downloaded straight from the camera or the card can be removed and inserted into an adapter in your computer. Images can then be saved on the hard drive, written to a disc, or printed for storage. The memory card can be reformatted and used over and over again. You may need to buy imaging software compatible with both your camera and your computer if it was not included in the package when you bought them.

It is important to remember that if the images are to be printed in a magazine they must be saved at 300 dots per inch (dpi) and at a size that will make them usable to the publisher. With the latest compression techniques, this is usually not a problem until the image needs to be larger than a single page. At that point, problems of quality can occur and it may be necessary to consider using a different media.

REVIEW

- ■ *Choose the right film for the job.*
- ■ *Double check your ASA dial before you shoot.*
- ■ *Only up-rate the whole roll and don't forget to label it.*
- ■ *Magazines will only accept finer grain films or 300dpi digital files.*

PUSHME-PULLYOU

It is possible to up-rate, or push, the effective speed of a film by increasing the ASA rating on the dial on your camera (if it has one), to the one stated on the film canister. This is useful in low light conditions when you may want to shoot some fast action and need an extra stop or two. It must be done at the start of the roll and the speed recorded on the roll when you remove it at the end. You will suffer a loss of quality if you do this, but it will only be noticeable if you push more than one stop. Remember: You must tell your processor at what speed you have rated your film so they can adjust the developing time accordingly.

Digital images are stored on a compact flash card or micro-drive that slots into the side of the camera. These vary in the amount of memory they offer from 16MB to 1GB and should be kept in the camera or stored in their own dust-free case.

Chapter 2
Basic Camera Techniques

COMPOSITION

When you have decided on your location and are happy with it, the next choice to make is how to compose the image in the viewfinder. The key to good composition is simplicity. Bear in mind that your initial view may not be the best and look for alternatives. The easy bit is pressing the shutter, so don't rush into it before thinking through how you want your picture to turn out. Everyone has their own way of seeing and if you asked five people to take a photograph of the same subject you would end up with five totally different images.

Most cameras produce an oblong image, so you have a choice of holding it level for a landscape orientation, or upright for portrait. Then choose the angle of the shot. If you want or have time for only one picture, then it's usually best to shoot a front three-quarters view of the car. This view shows off the shape well and it's the view that most people will recognize. When you are choosing which angle of view you want, think about any particular design details that stand out on the car and that you might want to highlight. If the grille is fantastic, then a more head-on angle might look good; if it's a convertible, a more side-on view might work better. Even the back of the car may be the best feature—for example, a 1950s car with spectacular tail fins. Next think about height. People are used to seeing cars at eye-level, so why not try something different? You could lie on the ground to look up at your subject, or look for a window or a bridge you might shoot from. In Monte Carlo, for example, there are plenty of places where you can look down on the cars due to a track that winds through the steep streets, making it an exciting place to shoot.

Another way to change the image is with a different lens. By changing a lens, you change the angle of view. A telephoto lens restricts the angle of view but enlarges the subject in the frame; a wide-angle lens increases the angle of view but reduces the size of the subject in the frame.

Long telephoto lenses—135-300mm —flatten perspective and are useful to crop into an area and exclude the background or compress it to heighten its effect. They can also be used to limit the depth of field effectively. Choosing a large aperture for a shorter depth of field renders the foreground and background unsharp, which draws the viewer's eye to the sharply focused subject.

Wide angles—18-35mm—exaggerate perspective and distort straight lines when used up close, but they can be very dramatic. With a wide lens, it's important to keep

1. 35mm lens. You need to choose your lens to suit your subject and location. Great sky but the car is lost. **2.** 50mm lens. Still too far away; without a long lens it would be better to move closer to the car. **3.** 70mm lens. Changing the lens alters the perspectives within the viewfinder. **4.** 200mm lens. From this distance ,flattened perspective and a narrow depth of field focus the eye onto the car large in the frame. **5.** 300mm lens. Cropping in on the car can be a way of hiding unsightly areas at your location or picking up particular design details.

Opposite: Think about getting some height to shoot from. This shot of a Porsche 917 was taken from a bridge over the pit lane at Silverstone racetrack. 80mm f11 1/125 second.

Right: Use depth of field as a way of pinpointing or hiding the main focus of interest in the picture. 180mm f4 1/250 second.

Far right: By shooting with a large aperture you can choose your focal point highly selectively. 180mm f4 1/250 second.

the camera level or the picture can look out of balance. Also, pay attention to what sneaks into the background as your angle of view will be enormous. Later on in the book there is an example of how *NOT* to shoot a car, and creeping into the background is a set of ladies' toilets!

Most portraits of people and cars are shot on a medium telephoto lens of around 70–135mm. This type of lens will draw the subject into the frame without flattening the features too much.

Choose a lens that will make the best use of your location. There's no point shooting at Niagara Falls if you shoot on a 300mm lens and crop tight in on the car. On the other hand, if all you've got is a patch of clean gravel in a crowded parking lot the same 300mm lens might be perfect. Remember you can use the right lens to select only the section of the view that you want. Look around and line up your subject carefully to make sure you only have what you want in the frame.

How to position the car in the frame will depend on the elements you want to include. The frame is made up of a foreground, middle distance, and background. Getting these elements in harmony with each other will balance the shot and give it strength.

The Golden Section is a grid of imaginary lines vertically and horizontally in thirds across the frame that guides the eye to the main point of interest. 180mm f 8 1/30 second.

Linear perspective can be used to great effect when shooting cars with a large depth of field by allowing a road or converging lines to draw the eye into the frame to suggest distance. 24mm f16 1/60 second.

THE RULE OF THIRDS

Your primary subject need not be centered in the photograph. The eye is also drawn to a point approximately one-third in and one-third up from the bottom. Photographers call this the rule of thirds, and it can provide variety and increased impact to your pictures.

There are other such tricks that can be very effective. For a good idea of how a shape or a pattern will work in the frame, close one eye and half-close the other. This will cut out your 3-D vision and you will only be able to see the main elements in the picture. You can change the picture's emphasis by cropping with the viewfinder, or after you have processed the image.

Discovering a repetitive pattern or shape is an effective way of isolating your subject from reality. These pictures can be shot using a standard or telephoto lens and a small aperture to flatten the image and give it the maximum depth of field. You can also open up the aperture fully and focus right in on a part of the image. A long lens compresses the different elements of a picture giving them similar emphasis in the frame and reducing perspective or sense of depth. Most SLR cameras will have a button next to

the lens that will show you exactly what depth of field you have at any aperture before you shoot.

The use of symmetry and asymmetry can make for interesting and unusual photos, so look out for shapes you can use in or around your chosen location to add a secondary element. Be careful not to introduce a conflict of interest, however. Don't get caught trying to shoot your car in front of a fabulous palace, because you will only end up with a bad photo of both.

Color is another tool for enhancing your photo's impact. You can use colors to great effect by looking for contrasts or a wide spectrum, or by limiting how much color you utilize. A red car on a dusky-grey, empty street will stand out much more than in the middle of a parking lot at midday.

Last, and by no means least, there is texture. Cars are all pretty much sleek and shiny subjects, so why not find a background that is different, rough, and jagged—like a junkyard,

a stone or gravel quarry, or a lumberyard. All of these make great locations because they are unusual, interesting, and have great texture.

Keep your eyes and your mind open for new ideas. Look at books and magazines to see how other photographers do it and learn from them. Remember rules are there to be broken and sometimes ignoring all this in a deliberate way comes up with interesting results.

LIGHT

Lighting is what will finally make or break your photo. It is the paint for your canvas and how you use and understand it is fundamental to success with your pictures. The amount, quality, direction, and color of light all have dramatic effects on how your picture will look.

Incredibly, the best time of day to shoot cars is five minutes after the sun has set on a cloudless summer evening. Your subject will be lit by a soft warm glow that shows every angle and shape and the body panels will shine like liquid metal. You'll have to work fast because the light levels will be rapidly dropping, so it's best to put in some preparation beforehand.

The time of day and the weather are the two critical factors that will affect what type of light you have to shoot with. Sometimes you can wait, sometimes you can't. If you can plan your shot, you might want to visit your chosen location at different times of the day. Take a compass with you so you can work out how the sun will move across the area.

On a cloudless day, the sunlight gets harsher the higher the sun gets in the sky, and by midday, it blasts off everything causing hard shadows and very high contrasts. This is not ideal if you are looking for a subtle image, but great if you need the light for a high shutter speed and don't care about where it's coming from. In the morning and

Opposite: Colors have a major part to play in your evolving composition. 200mm f8 1/8 second. **Left:** This panoramic shot of an Austin Healey was shot after the sun had gone down on a clear, summer evening when the light was soft and warm. 35mm f22 1/2 second.

Shooting against the light is a good option when the sun is low in the sky. Be careful to shield the lens from flare. 180mm f5.6 1/125 second.

afternoon the angle of the light is more oblique, highlighting textures and casting longer shadows, which totally changes the mood of the scene. This is a good time to shoot against the light, or with it reflecting in the side of the car, and makes a much more interesting image.

As clouds come over, shadows diminish as the light diffuses and gets softer and less contrasting. A bright, overcast day is almost as good for shooting cars as the dusky glow. It's a lot more predictable and lasts longer. It's good for shooting interiors, engines, and other details, as they will be lit evenly and show off their shape well. It's also fine for action as you won't have to worry about direction of the sun and problems with shadows, so that fantastic corner you found and couldn't use with the sun behind it is now an option.

SHOOTING AT NIGHT

As the light goes from the sky, so does the color from the land. Other light sources start to take over. Streetlights, headlights, and storefronts all add to the fading light in the sky as does the rise of the moon. Even the stars are usable light when it comes to taking photographs.

Using a long lens is okay if you are sure that the tripod can't move at all and you are wearing your running shoes. Choose a brightly lit store with neon lights or a similar spectacular display and compose your shot with the car 10-20 feet away from the tripod in the foreground.

Check the exposure using your (TTL) meter or, if you have one, a hand-held meter. Choose an aperture with a depth of field that will make everything sharp. On a wide-angle lens this will be above f8, and on a standard lens, f16. You should adjust your meter to give you the shutter speed. It's a good idea to double the speed suggested by your TTL meter when shooting at night. This could be anything from 1 second to 30 seconds. You may need to turn your shutter dial to B, which will keep the shutter open as long as the button is pressed, or T, which will open and close it each time. It's also a good idea to use a cable release to operate the shutter to prevent jogging the camera.

To be assured that you get the shot, you may have to shoot a range of exposures. This is called bracketing. To do this, change only the shutter speed, leaving the aperture set the same throughout. Typically, a good bracket would double the length each time—e.g., 2 seconds, 4 seconds, 8 seconds, 15 seconds, and 30 seconds is about right for ASA 100 film.

Now you'll need to fill in the foreground, including your subject, with a pop or two from your flash gun to neutralize the colored light on the car.

Set the flash one stop under the aperture and press the shutter for your first exposure. With the shutter open, run in front of the lens and manually fire the flash gun off two or three times at different parts of the car, making sure to keep moving and not point the flash back at the camera. Because the exposure is so long, you will not appear on the film but the light from the flash will balance the subject against the background.

If you want to shoot away from the city lights, under the moon and the stars, you will have to be patient. Using a faster film will help to reduce your exposure time but be

Best results at night come from shooting a long exposure on an SLR camera with a wide-angle or standard lens fixed to a tripod with a pop from your flash gun. 50mm f8 4 seconds.

Use fill-in flash set at one or two stops under the aperture to neutralize artificial lighting in the foreground and let the background go. 20mm f8 1 second.

prepared for shutter speeds of up to 30 minutes at f11 for ASA 200 with a full moon. At this shutter speed, you will even have movement of the stars in the sky!

ARTIFICIAL LIGHT

There are only two ways to go with artificial light: with it or against it. What I mean is that you can try to neutralize the weird colors it will create on your film by either using your flash gun or filters, or just let the weird colors happen and maybe turn them into a feature of the photograph.

The strange colors are there because of the temperature of the light and the light scale is measured in Kelvins (K). You can buy a special color meter to measure them, but the meters are expensive and quite tricky to use.

Color temperature is best understood by imagining that you are looking into a brightly lit house while standing on a dark street at dusk in the wintertime. Everything looks slightly orange and warm, but if you go into the house and look out of the window, the landscape will look a little blue and cold. This is because your eyes have color balanced themselves to suit the environment you are in. If you were to take a picture of the same scenes the difference would be greatly exaggerated with the blue and oranges taking over the picture.

Here's a chart to show you what happens to daylight film in different colored lighting and how to correct it, if you want to:

Type of Light	Color Temperature	Effect	Correction Filter
Household	2500K	yellow	blue, 80B
Studio	3200K	orange	blue, 80A
Fluorescent	none	green	magenta, FLD
Street	1800K	orange/green	blue, 82A

The filter numbers shown are Kodak Wratten filters, which carried in-stock at most camera stores.

Light color is more of a problem if you are shooting on transparency film. To allow for such situations, it is possible to get slide film balanced for tungsten light. Print film has a very broad latitude and most colors can be corrected in the printing stage.

Taking a relaxed attitude about light colors can work fine for car photos but not for people, as there's nothing so strange as folk with green skin and hair unless you've just met an alien. (No doubt many of the images claimed to be extraterrestrial result from uncompensated environmental effects on the film.) Always pop a bit of flash into a scene with people in it if you are shooting in artificial light. Note that many fluorescent strip bulbs are now daylight balanced, so it might be worth checking the bulb before you go slapping filters on your camera.

REVIEW

- **Don't shoot from head height if you can avoid it.**
- **Choose your lens to match your location.**
- **Look for repetitive pattern and shape.**
- **Use perspective and symmetry.**
- **The best light is at dawn and dusk.**
- **Check any tricky exposures with a hand-held light meter.**
- **Use a tripod.**

FILTERING THE LIGHT

Filters can be a handy way of enhancing your pictures if used well. Excluding that purple filter with the hole in the middle you saw in the bargain bin at your local photo store, there are some really good filters that can help balance the highlights and shadows and reduce contrast. The most useful is the graduated grey filter, which will give you some detail in the sky on a cloudy day or intensify that blue. A polarizing filter will also punch up a blue sky or reduce reflections on water and glass—but it may create crazy undesirable patterns on toughened windshields, so use it with care.

If you are shooting in shadow or just want to warm up your pictures, a pale orange filter called an 81EF will do the trick, and if you have to shoot under neon light, an FLD filter will stop your photos from going green. There are different sizes and systems, so make sure any filters you do buy are compatible with your lenses and Place them in a soft case because they scratch easily.

Left: As a rule of thumb, when shooting classic cars, look for a background older than the car itself. MGTC at Brooklands. 50mm f22 1/8 second. **Above:** With newer cars, look for something as modern as possible. BMW Z1 200mm f5.6 1/125 second.

LOCATION, LOCATION, LOCATION

This is one of the catchphrases for the real estate business but it could have been written for car photographers. Finding the right location is the key to a successful shoot. The right location will have a sympathetic background. It will have a key feature that will suit the type of car you are shooting. Simplicity plays a large role, but you must be guided by the type of car, phot purpose, and of course, what's available.

An ideal location will have space to move the car around to view its best angles and enough space for you to get back from the car to use your portrait or long lenses. The location should be quiet both in terms of people and traffic. There is nothing more

Left: Be creative. Shot in a parking lot in five minutes because we had to, this simple shot of a BMW 2002 worked well in the magazine. 135mm f8 1/60 second. **Above:** This beautiful 280SL Mercedes was photographed inside a reservoir on a hazy day, giving it excellent diffused light and a simple background. 180mm f11 1/15 second.

irritating than being about to shoot when someone walks through your frame or, even worse, parks in it.

Your chosen background should be simple and the area immediately surrounding the car should be uncluttered. This allows the line of the car to be uninterrupted and showits shape. Avoid telephone poles, traffic signs, overhead power lines, and any other thing that will lead the eye away from your subject. This also applies to things that you can do something about, such as movable trash cans and other parked cars. If you explain what you are doing, most people won't mind moving their cars if there's space to do so.

Next look for a good surface. Cars look lousy on grass, so avoid it. Also avoid painted lines, puddles, drain covers, curbs, and mixed surfaces where one changes to another,

All photographers edit their photos because they don't want to show all their bloopers, but also to give the pictures a certain feel and make them work together as a set.

e.g., pavement becoming dirt. Go for a firm surface. New tarmac, paved brick or stone, cobblestone, gravel, a dry dirt road, and even new white concrete can look good, if clean. If you are shooting on gravel make sure you pick up any cigarette butts or other small litter that might come back to haunt you later on.

The whole area around your car should ideally be made up of one type only. This is even more true when shooting from a height. The surface surrounding the car can become your key feature, e.g., cobblestones or stone paving. If you have time sweep the area with two or three buckets of water. This will pick up some light and give your picture a bit more depth. This technique is particularly effective for dusk or night shots.

As part of your location research, discover in which direction the light is moving. If you have the assistance of location finders, they will always report back to the photographer with shots of the site and compass bearings to show which way the sun will move over the scene.

Don't try to shoot in part sun and part shade on a sunny day. This provides too much contrast for the film to handle and you may lose detail and have difficulty choosing the right exposure. You may find that waiting a while for the sun to move will make all the difference for your picture, so be patient. However, it could make it worse, so be prepared to move quickly if you have to.

REVIEW

- *Choose a simple background.*
- *If you are shooting a classic car, use locations as old as the car or older.*
- *Take care finding the right base for the car to park on.*
- *Watch for the changing light.*

EDITING YOUR PICTURES

One of the skills that you will learn through experience is how to edit your photographs, and it's a good discipline to get into. If you've just come back from a weekend's racing with 20 rolls of film, your friends will soon lose interest if you make them wade through hundreds of out-of-focus pictures and images of your feet. They will be impressed, however, if you show them the 20 best images carefully selected from the pile.

Certain types of photography will need more or less editing due to how many variables affect the shoot. A bright day at an outdoor car show will need a lot less editing than a gloomy winter day at the track. Accepting the variables, the number of good shots you can expect from a roll of 36-exposure film is called the hit rate. It's an important concept to grasp and apply because it helps you determine how much film you need to shoot to get the pictures you need. With a digital camera, you can edit as you go, raising your hit rate to near 100 percent.

At a quiet location where you have plenty of time, the only variable you should have is exposure. If you are shooting transparency film you may be bracketing to ensure you get it right, so allow three or four frames for each shot. This means your hit rate will be about eight or ten shots per film.

This rate decreases if you shoot some action out on the road or track. With the possible movement of the car and camera, your hit rate can decrease to four to six sharp images on a roll. If you add to this poor light or other factors such as heavy traffic or a bumpy road, you may be lucky to get a single frame you are happy with. This is a law of averages, so if you know the odds are against you, shoot more film.

The best images will usually leap out of the roll as you look at them. If you are looking at transparencies use a loupe (a small magnifier on an eyepiece that will allow you to see what is sharp and un-sharp) and a light-box or a shaded window. Go through and put to one side all images that are out of focus, blurred, over- or underexposed, or for one reason or another fall into the blooper category. Don't throw these away just yet.

Choose your favorites, selecting a good mix of different angles and types of shot, to make up a set of pictures to print, archive, or send to a magazine. When you are happy with these selections, go back to the bloopers pile and look at them again. Are there any shots in there that still work, despite being technically incorrect? As in any art, beauty is in the eye of the beholder, so if you like that blurry weird shot of your foot with the race car on it keep it and try to work out how you did it so you can do it again (and possible even better).

Now throw out the rest or at least put them in the attic to go through when you are 98 years old and art has a new meaning!

This shot suffers from bad flare from the taillight and was initially edited out only to be included in the final choice as something different. 50mm f5.6 1/30 second.

REVIEW
- **You can't keep every photo you've ever taken.**
- **Edit as you go with a digital camera.**
- **In challenging situations with a low hit-rate shoot more film.**
- **Choose a variety of angles.**

Chapter 3
Preparing the Car for the Shoot

Despite its convenience, a mechanical car wash doesn't get your car very clean. A jet wash is better, finished off by hand.

Some cars are blanketed in heated garages and polished weekly while others have to face the school run or work everyday. No matter what their background, this section will show you how to get the best out of your subject in preparation for its moment of glory in front of the lens.

WASH AND GO!

Wash the car with water and a sponge, starting at the roof and working your way down. Dry it off with a chamois. This will remove most crud, but you might need to use a little car shampoo or glass cleaner to get rid of oil or stubborn bug marks. You don't need to polish it if you don't want to, as it will make little difference for the picture and it's hard work. Use a stiff brush to attack the wheels and get in between any spokes. There are some special cleaners to remove brake dust but be careful as they are not suitable for all wheel types, so read the label carefully. Wipe the tires with water, or if they are going a bit grey, glass cleaner works well if it's wiped on with a cloth. Check the treads for pebbles and pry them out with a small screwdriver or a key. Wipe the glass with a clean chamois inside and out.

Make sure all the doors, the hood, and the trunk are properly shut and that the windows are all the way up. When shooting a convertible, put the windows all the way down, the top down, and, if there is a cover for the top, make sure that it is properly fitted.

Rare Vinyl

Inside, vacuum out the footwells and the seat crevices. Give the floor mats a good shake and, if they are dusty, a wipe with a damp cloth. You will probably remove them when you shoot the interior, so check that the carpet underneath is clean too. Remove map books, tapes and CDs, mobile phones, and anything that wasn't there when the car came out of the showroom.

Wipe over the vinyl dash and door panels if they need it. There are vinyl cleaners that work well on interiors and external plastic bumpers, but don't use them on the day of the shoot as they tend to leave the surface hyper-shiny and it will need a few days to look normal again. Leather needs to be treated with respect. There is a wide range of hide creams and special treatments for restoring it to condition; in the short term, a clean, slightly damp cloth will remove most dirt and stains.

Level up the seats and headrests to make sure they are the same height, and carefully straighten the rearview mirror. If they are not retractable, tidy the seatbelts onto their hooks or hide them under the seat completely. If neither of these options looks good, lay them neatly across the seat base. Try to leave the steering wheel the right way up so that any spokes look even from outside. Finally, check that the interior lights go off when you close the door.

Windsurfers Do It Standing Up

If they come off easily, remove any window stickers. They draw the eye in to them like a beacon and muck up the line of the car. This goes for bumper stickers, too. But if it's not your car, remember to check with the owners to make sure they don't mind. Stubborn stickers will usually come off with hot soapy water, but if they are really stuck onto the windshield use a little nail polish remover on a cloth. Becareful not to get it on any painted surface as it may

Everything that could be wrong in one picture: Cluttered background, tires with stones in, facing out, wide angle lens close up and not level, door and trunk open, stuff visible inside, window half-open and someone walking through the frame near painted lines on the ground, UGHH!

Just around the corner, this aircraft hanger made a clean and simple background to show off the SLK's great lines. 200mm f5.6 1/30 second.

remove that, too! Last, take out removable stickers or license plates and their holders, but keep them handy in the glove box in case the law needs to see them.

Itchy Scratchy

Dents, dings, and scratches can be problematic if you have to shoot the whole car and can't hide them behind an owner or a carefully placed prop. Choose an angle with the light behind you so that any shadow or highlight is minimized or—even better—only shoot the good side. Small scratches can be touched up carefully and, when polished, can all but disappear. Broken or dented license plates look tacky so get new ones made up if you have the time. If the radio antenna is broken, see if you can coax it back into its casing. Hopefully you'll never photograph a car with all of these things wrong.

You won't be able to do everything for every shoot, but it's good practice to know where the pitfalls lie and often only one or two changes will make all the difference.

REVIEW

- ■ **Make sure the car is clean.**
- ■ **Wipe the tires and plastic bumpers.**
- ■ **Remove any window or bumper stickers with owner's permission.**
- ■ **Put the radio antenna down.**
- ■ **Close windows on a sedan.**
- ■ **Open windows on a convertible.**

SHOOTING DETAILS

Tricky little buggers. They lull you into a false sense of security and *Whammo!* Muck up your whole shoot. Just why did the hood on that white Corvette at the summer show come out looking like it was really a dull grey and shot at night?

The reason why some details are so difficult to get right is often tied to exposure problems. If you fill the frame with a beautiful black leather interior and just push the button, the picture will be wildly overexposed. The camera's light meter will be fooled by the low light reflected and overcompensate the exposure setting. You'd have a similar problem shooting the hood detail on the white Corvette, but this time the light meter would assume brilliant light and the picture would come out underexposed and overdark.

Meter readings are designed to give you an average so if you follow them exactly they will make both a white subject and a black subject look grey.

The way to get around these problems is to take your time and set up the shot properly. Use a tripod and a hand-held meter for your light reading. Point the meter back at the camera from the subject, which will measure the light falling on it. Next, take another reading pointing the light meter a way from the camera and close to the subject; this will measure light

Above: Shot from this side it's a disaster area, but you wouldn't know this damage was there if you turned the car around and shot the other side. **Below:** You don't need to go crazy like these guys at the Pebble Beach Concours and clean the underneath of the car. Only clean the parts of the car that you will see through the lens.

Interiors are nearly always best shot using natural light, camera on a tripod, and a long exposure. Play around with your composition. Try shooting through the sunroof or using the door halfclosed to frame the picture.
28mm f11 1/4 second.

reflected back from the subject. With both readings in hand, set your camera halfway between.

Here's an example:

1st reading meter pointing	
toward camera	f11 at 1/4 second
2nd reading meter pointing	
away from the camera	f11 at 1 second
Set the camera to	**f11 at 1/2 second**

If you only have a TTL or automatic light meter, you'll need to work out an average reading to get your correct exposure. To do this, find a patch of evenly lit grey asphalt or evenly lit grass and point your camera at it to fill the viewfinder. Make sure that the area you are pointing your camera at is lit the same way as your intended subject, i.e., in sun or in shade. Don't mix the two or your average reading will be wrong. Take a meter reading through the lens and use the same reading for shooting your detail.

If the camera is automatic, you may need to hold down the shutter button to retain the same exposure setting, but be careful that this doesn't affect your autofocus as well.

If this all sounds a bit complicated there is a general rule for bright subjects close down the lens one stop and for dark subjects open up one stop. This works well in shade or on a cloudy day, but if you are shooting in full sun make that adjustment two stops.

Interiors

There are always many great details in the cabin of a car. Take a good look around and discover all those features the designers put in to wow new owners.

When shooting a convertible, it's fine to let the sun in to liven up the image, but watch out for the shadows. With a sedan you don't want the sun anywhere in the image. Move into the shade, create a shadow with a reflector, or just turn the car so that the sun doesn't get into your shot. If it does, it will cause bright highlights and deep shadows that will detract from the detail you are trying to show off. It's a good idea to warm up your interior shots in the shade by using a warm-up filter in front of the lens. Otherwise the film can go a little blue.

Pop in a bit of flash one stop under for that cloth interior, but don't use it on leather or paint work as it will give you nasty highlight reflections. If you do use flash on a dark cloth interior or to fill in the dark footwells, pick over the photographed area and carefully remove any specks of dust or dirt, as these will reflect the flash and leap out at you in the photo.

If you don't have a tripod and want to shoot an interior, lean the camera carefully into the top corner of the door jam. This will give you a steady platform to shoot from—don't forget to ask the car's owner first.

Shooting the dash is easy on a convertible with the roof down but harder on a sedan. Climb into the back seats and either rest your camera between the headrest and the roof or squeeze it between the seat and the headrest. This saves all the bother of trying to squeeze your tripod into the back of the car and still gives you great lighting and a steady platform to use longer shutter speeds than you could with a hand-held.

If you want to shoot the sound system or in-car television in operation, you'll need to use a longer exposure to get those LEDs to show up or to avoid getting lines on the TV. Shutter speeds less than 1/8 second should be okay for the TV, but longer duration may be needed for the in-dash stereo, as LEDs are not very bright and don't show up well on film.

The same goes for any dashboard lighting. A good time to shoot your interior with the lights on is that golden half-hour after sunset. You'll need to use a long exposure on a wide lens and an aperture of more than f11 to get everything sharp. You might want to zoom in for a close-up if the instruments look good, but make sure your tripod is secure so you don't suffer any long-lens wobble during your exposure.

We covered how to make the cabin look its best in the "Preparing the Car" section, but it's a good idea to remind yourself of some of the main tips.

Black interiors will fool your camera light meter so don't forget to adjust your exposure or bracket a few frames either way to make sure you get the shot. 35mm f16 1/2 second.

Crop in close if an engine has a dirty battery or you need to hide any other anomalies under the hood. This car had a brand-new white battery that was highly distracting.
35mm f8 1/15 second.

REVIEW

- *Steering wheel straight with logo the right way up.*
- *Rearview mirror level and not reflecting anything distracting.*
- *Keys out of the ignition.*
- *Unless you are specifically shooting it, turn the stereo off.*
- *Tidy the seatbelts.*
- *Even up the seats so they look the same.*
- *Remove maps, phones, CDs, tapes, and garbage.*
- *Remove the floor mats.*
- *Check for dust on the dash and seats.*
- *Windows down on a convertible, up on a sedan.*

Engines

When you are shooting an engine, look carefully to see that you are in the optimum place to show off its features: Which is its best side? Is the hood support in the photo? Is there any clutter sneaking into the side of the frame?

Keep it simple. Move in on the engine bay so you don't see anything outside and not too much of the underside of the hood. Have a friend hold the hood so you don't have the support cutting across the picture.

Use natural lighting and a long exposure with the camera on a tripod, instead of a flash as your main source of light to avoid harsh shadows. Use your flash gun to fill in one or two stops under the daylight exposure, if you need to, on a dull day. Another good tip is to tape a piece of white card or a reflector onto the underside of the hood. This will bounce light down onto the top of the engine and will show up well in chrome air filter covers or cam boxes. Make sure the reflector doesn't appear directly in the picture.

Clean up any oil drips or water marks around the hoses. These usually just wipe off with a damp cloth. If there is any untidy wiring, try to hide it by tucking it behind another component.

Most front-wheel-drive engines look best shot symmetrically from dead in front on a medium wide lens, such as a 35mm—but why not try shooting on a long lens from high up, like out of a window? This is a particularly good idea if the hood hinges at the front, or if the car is mid-engined, as it's tricky to get the camera into a good position. Looking down on the engine from a window or a ladder solves the problem.

If the oil cap has a name or a logo on it, turn it to get it straight. But don't forget to tighten it again afterward! There also may be writing on the cam boxes that you want to feature in a close-up. To highlight this, move around to the side of the car so that the sky reflects into it.

On older cars, it's possible to completely remove the hood either as one piece or in two sides. This gives great access, but be careful what you have in the background and that you are shooting the best side. When shooting pre-war cars, if you have to choose, go for the carburetor side becasue it is usually more interesting.

Wheels

One of the styling details that most affects the look of a car is its wheels. Concept cars at motor shows and fabulous styling drawings are always given huge wheels to make them look sexier, but these rarely make it through to production. A whole industry exists just to supply aftermarket alloy wheels for owners with steel wheels or those who fancy a change.

One of the first rules of photographing wheels is to get them really clean. Modern brakes kick out a pile of brake dust over time and this builds up in between the spokes and around the rims. Use a stiff soapy brush to get the loose stuff off, and you may need to use a special brake dust remover to get the wheels really clean. As mentioned earlier, be sure of the product's applications and directions', you don't want to damage the finish, just clean it.

If the lacquer or paint is chipped or coming off, you can buy touch-up kits from your local car accessory store to repair them. But if the rims have been curbed and are dented you may have to get them refinished by a specialist. In a pinch, place the damaged wheel on the opposite side, or see if there's a spare available with the same rim and tire. On older cars, this is a decent bet.

To get light into the engine bay, stick a piece of white card or ask a friend to hold it up under the hood while you shoot.

Look for any engine details while you have the hood open. Again, use the camera on a tripod and reflect more light in with your card if you need to. 50mm f4.5 1/30 second.

BATTERIES

Car batteries can cause all sorts of problems. In a classic car, if it is not an original or a period look-a-like, it may catch the eye with bright colors and modern graphics, so it's best to find an angle that allows you to crop them out of the picture altogether. The same goes when shooting in a new engine bay, which can often be let down by a battery that is dirty and terminals that are coated with acid deposits.

On most occasions a quick wash is enough to make them presentable and sometimes, as with wire wheels, it's not possible to get in between the spokes without removing them because they are tightly packed together.

A jet wash is a good way of getting the muck off but it's not recommended for older cars as the high-pressure water can get into body seams and moisture traps, creating a risk of rust in the future.

Next, think about what the wheel is standing on. Grass is still off limits unless you have to, as it breaks up the line of the tire and the car may sink into it. It is much better to look for solid ground. Avoid white lines, puddles, and dirty asphalt. Go for gravel, stone, cobblestone, or clean asphalt.

Make sure the wheel is the right way up, with any center logo dead straight. Turn the wheel away from the camera just enough to lose the edge of the tire, but not so far as to break up the circle of the rim. Check the tire for any stones caught in the treads and remove them with a key.

Choose an angle level with the center of the wheel. This works well because you usually don't have to worry about a background. Lie on the ground with a wide-angle lens and the camera rotated to shoot portrait and move in on the wheel until it nearly fills the frame. You should only have sky in the top of the frame and the car chopped off around the door mirror.

Another option is to look down on the wheel from above with a longer lens focusing on the center. This is good for wire wheels with a spinner in the middle because it shows off the depth and shape well.

Body Details, Badges, Etc.

Shooting details on the body is one of the hardest things to do well as panels can act like a convex mirror seeing everything all around you.

So when you move in for a close-up you must be aware of what is reflecting in the panel you want to focus on. Typically, it's the photographer, camera, and tripod that you see in silhouette and just like seeing your own shadow in the frame it's not very professional. This is at its worst shooting a dark-colored car with a curved panel or chrome bumper. Mid-tones, such as red, yellow, and silver are the most forgiving colors to shoot; while dark blue, dark green, and black are the worst.

There are a number of ways to reduce your reflection or sometimes even avoid it altogether:

Techniques for Reducing Reflection

1. Choose a longer lens or zoom in from six or eight feet away. The further you are away from the panel, the smaller your reflection will be.

2. Hide behind a reflector with just the camera poking out.

3. Make sure you are reflected only at the harshest angle of the curved panel; at the corner of a chrome bumper, you will only appear as a dot rather than a line (if shot from the side).

4. Use a little dulling spray to remove your reflection. This is a light wax that that has its origins in the movie industry and doesn't damage paintwork or chrome. It comes in an aerosol and is quite tricky to use. Spray in short bursts from about eight inches and keep your hand moving just like you were painting the car. When you want to remove it, just wipe it with a dry cloth or use a little glass cleaner. Remember to ask permission of the owner before you use it.

Small maker's badges need to be shot with a macro lens on a tripod. Use a small aperture and a large depth of field. When using a close-up lens, focusing becomes far more critical and it's important to use your depth of field preview button, if you have one, to ensure everything is sharp. If the badge is metal, it's easy to give it a bit of a lift by reflecting some white card into it.

Headlights are another good detail to shoot. Turn on to the parking lights so you get a bit of a glow showing. Low and hight beams are usually too bright for the camera to handle and will muck up your exposure. You can also turn on the hazard warning lights to add a bit more color but you will need to time your shooting to coincide with the flashes.

A careful detail shot can sometimes end up as the lead image in a magazine feature. 35mm f4.5 1/30 second.

Look for details that tell the story of the car. This leaping cat is from the hood of a MK2 Jaguar. 70mm f8 1/15 second.

If you are shooting an angle that includes the lights, why not turn them on? Headlights need only be on their park setting or flashing during a long exposure otherwise they may be too bright. 70 mm f11 1/4 second.

Detail shots are often really graphic and good for messing around with on the computer or practicing new techniques. This is shot on Polaroid and printed onto cartridge paper after only ten seconds of development.

Use a hand-held meter to check difficult details such as light or dark bodywork. Hold the meter facing the camera at 45 degrees from the vertical to get an accurate reading.

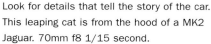

As with the headlights, the taillights look their best with something going on. Get a friend to put his foot on the brake pedal, or if you are alone put a brick on it to hold it down. Again, you can use the hazard lights or indicators to step up the action.

These photos look their best in low light, at dusk or dawn, where they take on an eerie glow with long exposures. You can activate the lights just to put some color in the picture if you are shooting on a dull day.

Big, beefy exhausts are so low to the ground on most cars that they have to be shot from above, so look out for what's underneath. Race car tail pipes are much easier, as they tend to come out higher up and give you more freedom to decide your angle. They are also often contorted into fabulous shapes at the manifold and make for great surreal close-ups.

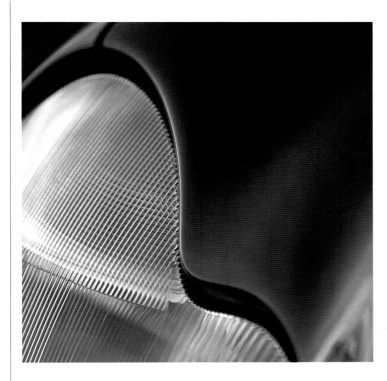

If you can wait until the sun has set on a clear evening you will be rewarded with the perfect light to shoot your details. But don't take too long—you may only have a few minutes to work with. 50mm f4 1/30 second.

REVIEW

- ■ *Use a hand-held light meter when shooting interiors.*
- ■ *Find an average reading through your TTL meter.*
- ■ *Use a tripod in daylight with long exposures.*
- ■ *Turn lights on when shooting them.*
- ■ *Look out for your own reflection in chrome close-ups.*
- ■ *Get wheels really clean.*

Think about new angles to shoot from. Not all your detail shots have to be close-ups—why not crop into the car from a distance to highlight what you want to show? 70mm f11 1/8 second.

Chapter 4
Action Photographs

Each time this Mercedes W154 came into Casino Square in Monte Carlo, a plume of flame shot from its exhaust as the driver momentarily lifted his foot off the throttle. 300mm f4.5 1/500 second.

To photograph the essence of a subject, you need to catch it at the "decisive moment." So said one of the greatest photographers of all time, Henri Cartier-Bresson. Although he wasn't a car photographer, he knew that to get the best photo you needed to put the subject in its element and be patient.

The element for the car is the moving road and even though you may get great static photos at shows or in well-chosen locations, the best way to get amazing shots of cars is to shoot them in action.

This section is split up into the different types of action shots that you can do and it explains exactly how to do them. It will cover panning, cornering, tracking from one car to another, and many other types of specialist action shots designed to create breathtaking photos. There is a level of difficulty scale next to each shot, with one being the easiest and ten the most difficult.

This section covers how to shoot at the racetrack and at other types of action events you might come across.

PANNING

Simple Panning Level of Difficulty: 5

This technique is one of the oldest in the book and the most developed of all. The car is shot from a side-on position, and the camera is swung in an arc to follow its movement. The shutter is pressed as it reaches the apex or just before. The effect is to freeze part, or the entire car, against a blurred background.

As long as you are not breaking the speed limit, it's okay to do this on a public road, but you must respect other drivers and always be aware of the safety implications.

Panning can be used for anything that's moving along a single plane, or diagonally toward or away from the camera. With the evolution of autofocus, it has been made a whole lot easier. You can use almost any lens for panning. We will be looking at both telephoto and wide lenses to get differing effects.

The rules here are all about shutter speeds. The idea is to freeze all or part of your subject against a blurred background to indicate speed. Usable speeds range from 1/8 to 1/500 second, and knowing when and how to use which speed is the key to great panning shots.

The decision of which shutter speed to use is based on four elements:

1. Your subject is speed.
2. How bright a day it is.
3. What your location is like.
4. How many chances you will get.

Not all cars will be able to zoom past the camera at a steady 60 miles per hour to create a perfect panning target. The road may be in a restricted speed area or the car incapable of more than 30-40 miles per hour.

Above left: Choosing your panning location is also important in getting a good hit rate. Ideally, you should look for somewhere with a wide-open smooth road, good visibility in both directions, space to get back from it on one side, with trees or another plain background close on the other side. This will give you the blurring speed effect, and the closer the background is to the road, the more blur you will get. **Above right:** It's a good idea to stop the car opposite and prefocus. It also helps if you can get hold of walkie-talkies to communicate with your driver and let him know when the road is clear.

A general fule for a sharp image with a long lens is the slower the car, the faster the shutter speed. For example, for a basic side-on pan with a 180mm lens about 25 yards away from the road:

Speed	Shutter Speed
10-30 miles per hour	1/250 second
30-50 miles per hour	1/125 second
50-70 miles per hour	1/60 second
70-150 miles per hour	1/30 second

This is to allow for lens shake as you swing the long lens in an arc for the panned shot. The faster you swing the camera, the smoother it gets, and the greater chance you have of getting a sharp photo.

There is a top limit too, and it actually begins to get harder again over about 150 miles per hour. At those speeds, your subject is around for a short length of time and you need to swing the camera fast, so the swing can get a little jerky. Also, it's no longer easy to find anything to practice on.

It's a good idea to pick up the car as early as possible as it approaches your shooting point so you can get into your swing early. Keep the car in the viewfinder with your finger resting lightly on the shutter button and, as it reaches your focus point, squeeze off two or three frames. Don't snap your finger onto the button as this will only create a wobble in your all-important panning swing and your pictures won't be as sharp as they could be. Carry your swing through after you have pressed the shutter, to keep the pan as smooth as possible.

1. 1/125 second—there is still quite a bit of detail in the fore- and background. **2.** 1/60 second—there is more blur in the background and the wheels. **3.** 1/30 second—the blur almost detaches itself from the sharp car; you will need to practice to hold the lens steady at this speed. **4.** 1/15 second—try a few at slower speeds and after some practice you will start to get parts of the car sharp. **5.** 1/4 second—this is great if you are in an unsuitable location and you don't need to see detail on the car; it just gives the essence.

This is easier with a motor-drive on your camera that will shoot off a few frames as you hold down the shutter button, but you will often find only one out of your burst of three is sharp, so it's quite possible to get by without one.

Another good tip is to line up your car statically on the road in the position you are going to shoot it and check your focus. This idea of prefocusing will appear again and again in this chapter, as you very often have to predict where the car is going to be at a certain moment and with these shots you'll have no time to adjust the focus at that point.

Tell your driver to pass through the same point each time, if possible, and maintain a steady speed. It's a great advantage if you have walkie-talkies so you can tell him to speed up, slow down, or of any danger ahead.

Use your common sense. Don't choose a busy road at rush hour, and find somewhere that your driver won't have to go miles to turn around and come back for another pass. Also avoid locations where you can only see the approaching car for a short time before you shoot, as this won't allow you enough time to achieve an even pan. At the right location you can shoot in both directions, halving the number of runs you need.

You don't have to shoot every time the car passes if it doesn't "feel" right or even have film in the camera to practice; you can just swing the camera back and forth at any moving traffic until you feel confident.

For these shots, you will need a good, patient driver who does what he is asked to do, as it may take as many as 10 or 20 drive-bys before you are reasonably sure that you got the shot. You will only waste

SAY "CHEESE"!

If you are shooting a four-seat convertible, why not get someone in the back seat to wave or smile at the camera as they go past.

Opposite: 1. Front three-quarters panning is harder than side-on as the car is now moving in two planes. Here, 1/125 second with a 135mm lens, there is lots of blur but the moment of opportunity is very short. **2.** 1/25 second. To help with your prefocusing look for something on the road that you can focus on—it might be a pebble or a crack in the asphalt—and use it to mark the point where you are going to press the shutter. If there is nothing remarkable, you can place a small stone on the side of the road to help you. **3.** 1/500th second. This would be almost pin-sharp on a longer lens, but still has plenty of movement in it and a much higher hit rate.

time and film if your driver goes too fast or can't drive through the point you need him to. Don't expect to be able to master this difficult technique right away. As with any of these skills, your abilities will get better the more you do it.

If you have an autofocus camera and lens, panning is one of the most effective shots you can do. It works well in evenly lit locations with little in the foreground, but you may discover that focusing manually gets you a higher hit rate.

The other automated function that can come unstuck is our old buddy exposure. You'll need to meter just as carefully for an action shot as you do for a static, for as the car gets closer and larger in the viewfinder the metering will be all over the place. There is no ideal direction of light, but be careful when shooting with the sun directly behind the camera as you may suffer from serious glare right at your shooting point. Exposure may also govern what shutter speed you can use. Your aperture and depth of field have very little effect on a side-panned photograph. The image is nearly flat and the background is blurred so you don't notice if it's not sharp.

If it's noon on a bright sunny day you may not be able to shoot slower than 1/125 second if your lens only stops down to f22. You may want to shoot faster, particularly if the car is going really quick, such as at a racetrack. You'll even get a slight blurring at 1/500 second, so try different speeds and find one you are happy with. If your heart is set on a slower speed than the light will allow, you can fit a neutral density (ND) filter to the front of the lens and this will knock one or two stops off your exposure.

There won't be so many options on a cloudy winter day and you may struggle to shoot faster than 1/60 second with your lens wide open at f2.8 or f4. Try to get a bit arty and slow the shutter speed down to 1/8 or 1/4 second. This will give you a greater depth of focus and lots of blur. You'll see the shape of the car with the colors all flowing into the background and sometimes a single element will emerge sharp amongst the maelstrom. This gives an atmospheric alternative to the usual panning shot and may get you out of a dark hole.

Don't forget that you can "push" your film one or even two stops if the light gets really dim, but you must rate the whole roll at the same speed, and don't forget to label it and tell the lab what you have done. Also, if your camera does not read the *dx* coding on the film to set the ASA automatically, don't forget to reset it back to the normal ASA for the next roll. Many rolls have been wasted by photographers not checking the ASA each time they load a film, so it's a good habit to get into.

The other factor that will play a part in which shutter speed you choose is how many times the car will be in a panning position. If you know that Mario Andretti is only going to do one tribute lap at a race meeting, you've got to get the shot. Take your time choosing your position and prefo-cusing. Set your camera to a high shutter speed, such as 1/250 or 1/500 second and double-check all your camera settings:

Settings Double-Check
- ASA
- Exposure
- Enough film left on the roll
- Battery power check

If you have an autowind camera, it's a good idea to shoot a couple of extra frames as the car passes so you have five or six to choose from.

Front Three-Quarters Panning
Level of Difficulty: 7

Of course, you don't have to wait until the car is level with you before you shoot. If you autofocus or prefocus at an earlier point you can get a front three-quarters panning shot. This is harder than the flat, side-on version as the car is traveling in two planes, but the effects can be dramatic.

Even though it will work well on a long telephoto lens, such as 180-210mm, it looks better on a medium telephoto of around 80-135mm. This is because you don't get so much of the flattening effect of the long lens and it shows off the depth of the front three-quarters angle.

To do this shot you will need to increase your shutter speed and move in closer to the passing car. Start at about 10 yards away from the road and prefocus about 20 yards away.

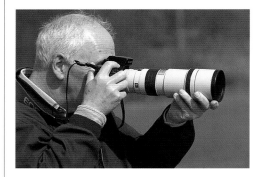

The best technique to stabilize the lens is to stand on level ground with your feet shoulder-width apart, facing the direction that the car is coming from. Hold the camera in your right hand and the far end of the lens with your left. Reverse this if you are left-handed. Keeping your feet firmly grounded, swing your body from the hips to follow the car, and keep the car in the viewfinder as it passes.

Zoom and panning is only possible with an autofocus zoom lens because requires the photographers to zoom out as the car comes toward them and there is no time for focusing.
70-200mm zoom 1/250 second f5.6.

With a 135mm lens, use 1/250-1/500 second shutter speeds and as you get better try a few at 1/125 second. This front three-quarters angle works very well from an elevated position. Look for a bank or a hill above the road so you can look down on the car as it comes toward you.

Zoom and Panning   Level of Difficulty: 8

Another version of the front three-quarters panning can only be done if you have an autofocus zoom lens. This is the sort of shot you see film cameramen shooting, but they have a guy standing next to the lens whose sole job is to look after the focusing. You can't do that so you'll need the autofocus to do it for you.

The idea is to keep the car in the center of the frame on a long telephoto zoom, such as a 70-200mm, and follow it all the way in. To do this, stand about 15 yards back from the road and pick up the car at your maximum zoom. As it gets nearer, zoom out at the same rate as the car is coming toward you. Use a shutter speed of 1/250 second to start with; if you are disappointed with the results you may need to go up to 1/500 second. This will give you a longer window of opportunity to shoot in and a greater variety of angles to choose from when you get your pictures back from the lab.

The three-quarters zoom and panning is one of the more difficult shots, so it may take a bit longer to master.

Short-Lens Panning   Level of Difficulty: 6

This is the sort of photo that you used to see taken by the great trackside snappers when "trackside" really meant it. They would stand with their toes on the edge of the corner and poke their lenses almost into the cockpit of the race cars as they went by. For safety reasons, race photographers are no longer allowed to do this but you can get some fantastic shots with this technique away from the track and out on the open road.

You can use any short or wide lens from 20mm to 50mm for this shot or a wide-angle zoom if you have one. Prefocus on the road about three to five yards away and practice your panning swing a few times.

This action is totally different from the other pans we have covered; it's more of a swipe than a pan. You'll need a shutter

1. Short lens panning needs to be shot at relatively higher shutter speeds to be assured of success. It is made harder by the very short time the car appears in the viewfinder. 20-35mm zoom 1/250 second f5.6. **2.** At slower speeds it's hard to get much sharper but still looks great. 20-35mm zoom 1/125 second f5.6. **3.** Set your shutter speed to 1/30 second or 1/60 second, and your flash gun to 1/2 stop under the daylight exposure reading. Pan the car into your firing point as usual, not forgetting to carry on the swing after you have shot to keep it smooth.

speed of about 1/250 second to get the majority in focus, but try 1/500 second as well.

The driver should not be going too fast—try about 30 miles per hour. If he's traveling much faster, it's very easy to miss the car altogether. It all happens very quickly when you are looking through the lens, so you may need to shoot a few extra runs to be sure you've got the shot, but it's worth the effort.

This shot also works very well on the inside of a bend or—even better—a hairpin

SAFETY

Make sure you are standing at least two yards back from the side of the road, at the inside of a corner on a wall, or behind a barrier where you are going to be safe from the traffic passing.

Top: This very slow panning shot is not expected to be sharp but it captures the mood and movement of the car as it races around the bend towards the camera. 70mm f16 1/8th sec

Above: You can get some great short-lens panning shots standing on the inside of a hairpin curve. It's also one of the safest places to shoot from because the car is going relatively slow and will spin away from you if the driver loses control. 35mm f11 1/15th sec

curve. The car remains at the same distance from the camera as it swings around the bend and it is in focus for much longer.

Another idea is to slow the shutter speed down and introduce a pop from your flash gun. This is particularly good when you are shooting in low light conditions and it's a shot widely used by rally photographers as they wrestle for an extra f-stop on dark forest stages.

If you are shooting with flash close up on a moving car, make sure you have somewhere to jump out of the way in case it startles the driver.

You could also try a short-lens zoom and pan, but this is a extemely difficult. To do it you'll have to zoom, pan, and fire the shutter in fractions of a second, so only try it if you have plenty of time and film left to experiment with.

Multiple-Car Panning **Level of difficulty: 9**

Again, this is way up there in the difficulty stakes, as you multiply all your variables by however many cars you have.

For this you'll need a very wide road, racetrack, or airfield runway if you intend on shooting more than two cars, and preferably a high viewpoint so you can see all the cars at once. The more cars you intend to shoot, the further away you will need to be. Be sure to allow a little extra space in the viewfinder because the shape of your convoy may change as it progresses in front of the lens. You will also need excellent drivers who are capable of pinpointing car placement.

Set the cars up statically in the positions you want to shoot them and make sure each driver knows where he is in relation to the cars on either side of him. This is important if you don't want one car to block another from the camera.

SAFETY IN FORMATION

The most important thing for the drivers to remember is not to make any sudden maneuvers when driving in close formation with other vehicles. Any braking, acceleration, or steering must be carried out slowly and smoothly to avoid a nasty accident. A good idea is to give the car at the front a walkie-talkie and get the others to take their lead and speed from the lead driver.

Keep it slow, around 40-50 miles per hour, and use a shutter speed of 1/250 second to decrease the amount of movement between the different cars. This shot is also better on a longer telephoto lens, such as 180-200mm, as it will compress your image and equalize the size of the car furthest from the camera to the one closest.

You'll need a depth of focus that will cover the full width of your car group, so this shot may not be ideal if you are not shooting on a bright day. Prefocus at a point one-third into the group at your static set-up before you start. This will give you the maximum depth of field for your aperture.

Set the cars off a long distance from where you are going to shoot to allow them to get into their positions. A staggered, overlapping formation is good to ensure no car can completely block another.

Due to the number of variables in this shot, you will need to shoot a few rolls before you can be sure you've got it. Be patient with your drivers. If they are not doing what you want, you probably haven't explained it properly. The more time you spend in planning at the start, the fewer runs they will need to make and the better your odds will be to get the shot.

The multiple-car pan is also a good shot to use at the start of a race as the cars tear away from the grid. Pan from up in a grandstand the first few seconds as the cars gather speed. Pick up on one car and follow it through the pack, letting all the others do their own thing. Choose a shutter speed of 1/250 second for the slow cars at the start or 1/60 second for cars at full race speed.

Multiple car panning sometimes happens before your very eyes on the racetrack where one car is overtaking another. Here, the speeds of the two cars will be different so you will need to choose one car to focus on and let the other go blurred as it races past. Front three-quarters pan 200mm 1/125 second f8.

TRACKING OR CAR-TO-CAR

This shot is the one you most commonly see in the car magazines, because you can do it almost anywhere and it's not too difficult to get great results. It involves three people—one driving the feature car, the photographer, and one driving the camera car. The feature car pulls up into an overtaking position just a few feet from the back of the moving camera car to get the picture, so you'll need good, confident drivers and a few runs before you get it just right.

It should be okay to do this on public roads as long as you obey all the safety rules and local laws. If you feel unsure, get a couple of buddies with walkie-talkies to stand at either end of the stretch of road and to warn the drivers of any danger, or make arrangements to shoot on a private road or track.

Get as low as you can for tracking photographs because much of the blur effect comes from the road. Get your camera car going at a steady speed and use signals to communicate with the car you are shooting. 28mm 1/60 second f8.

This is a safe, slow-speed shot so you will only be going 30-40 miles per hour.

The camera car needs to be a hatchback, 4 x 4, convertible, or sedan with a large, empty trunk big enough for the photographer to climb into. The best vehicles for this shot have self-leveling suspension and a powerful engine to get you up to speed or out of trouble quickly.

Don't attempt any of these shots in the rain, as spray from the camera car will soak you and your equipment, bury the feature car in a plume of water, and limit visibility for your drivers to a potentially dangerous level.

Front Three-Quarters Tracking
Level of Difficulty: 3

Location is key to making this shot work. You'll need a long, straight road that's not too bumpy and has little or no traffic. It will also need to be wide enough for two cars to drive side by side comfortably, with excellent forward visibility for both cars. Ideally, it will be open on one side to let the light in and closed in by a wall, hedge, or hill on the other. This will give you more speed effect than a totally open road.

The shot can be done safely on a two-lane highway, but watch out for faster traffic catching you up and pull in with plenty of time to spare. Be aware that some roads have a minimum speed limit as well as an maximum.

The positioning of the two cars is critical, so set up in a static formation before you start to make sure everyone knows what they are going to do.

Sit or lie in the back of the camera car and get as comfortable as you can with the camera pointing back toward your subject. You may want to put some padding down to cushion your body. If it's a hatchback, you can pull the rear seatbelts over and cross them around your chest for extra security. If you are in the trunk, sit with your back against the rear window and your legs hanging out of the car or kneel with your feet fully in the trunk. You can also shoot this shot out of the rear window of the car, but be careful not to get the camera car in the frame.

Clear out any trash or other stuff that might get in your way or fall out when you get moving, and arrange your camera gear around you so you can get more film or change a lens if you need it.

For this shot you will need a wide-angle lens—ideally a 35mm but a 28mm will be fine, too. During your static set-up, make sure you are pointing in the same direction that you will be shooting in so you can check your exposure as well as focusing.

A good starting shutter speed for this shot is 1/125 second, but with a smooth road and good driving you can get this down to 1/60 second or even 1/30 second for more blur effect.

You may find communications with the driver of the camera car difficult when you get moving, as the sound of your voice will get swept away by the wind and compete with the exhaust, so agree on your speed before you set off.

The same goes for your feature car. Work out a series of signals for him to slow down, speed up, or move left and right. Also tell the feature car driver what to do if he sees another car coming. In that event, he should ignore your signals, brake smoothly, and pull in behind the camera car. Discuss this situation with your driver and the feature car driver at the same time before you begin shooting. It may be helpful for the camera car driver to accelerate to make it easier for the feature car to pull in behind him.

One of the reasons for shooting at 30-40 miles per hour is that any faster speed will cause most tailgates to blow closed. You can prop the trunk or tailgate open with a monopod or tape the struts to stop them from moving if you keep getting hit on the head, but this usually means you are going too fast.

Start off together slowly, with your feature car following directly behind at the same speed and build up to 35 miles per hour. As you accelerate, you may need to hold on tight and make sure none of your gear rolls out onto the road.

In a car with a trunk, open the panel in the back seats so you can talk to your driver. Prop the trunk lid open with a tripod or tie it up to stop it from blowing down as you get going on your front three-quarters tracking shot.

Wave your feature car up into overtaking position after checking it's safe to do so. The feature car should be only about ten feet away and traveling at exactly the same speed as you are in the camera car.

Try to get as low as you can to the road, as this will accentuate the blur and feeling of speed. Don't drop your camera! If you have a strap, wrap it around your wrist if you feel unsure about it. Raise your camera up to your eye, either resting on your elbows or your stomach if you are lying down. Check your focus and fire off a few frames.

Your worst enemy now will be bumps in the road. Tell your driver to avoid them at all costs because you won't be able to shoot and may bang your face on the back of the camera or the floor of the car. For insurance it's good to drive the stretch of road where you'll shoot beforehand to look for bumps and ways to avoid them. If there's one that can't be avoided, have your driver warn you with a signal so you can brace yourself and the equipment.

Try to be ready to shoot on the best bit of your chosen road with trees or other background in it to add to the sense of movement. If there's a particular object or backdrop you want to include, work out a way for your driver to signal you just before you reach it.

If you are shooting with the sun low in the sky, look out for the shadow of the tailgate creeping into your shot or onto the feature car. Make sure the driver of your feature car isn't wearing anything too bright or looking directly at the camera.

Head-On Tracking   Level of Difficulty: 3

This is the same technique but instead of the car following to one side, it moves back into a central position behind the camera car. It works well with a long-hooded car, such as a Jaguar XKE.

Your location for this shot still needs to be a quiet, straight road but it will now help to have trees on both sides to give an even-blurring effect. With some planning it is possible to shoot in brightly lit tunnels, but remember that the artificial

Opposite: If you are shooting from the back of another feature car, why not include part of it in your shot? 35mm 1/60 second f8.

Above: The key when shooting head-on tracking images is symmetry. If the feature car is not exactly behind the camera, the shot won't work. Shoot from a higher position out of the back of the camera car and carefully compose your image to be balanced side to side.
35mm 1/30 second f5.6.

lighting may cause your film to go all sorts of weird colors.

Keep your shutter speed set to 1/125 second or 1/60 second, but be careful with your focus and depth of field as you may need more than in the front three-quarters view. If the car has a long hood, you should only need enough depth of field to reach to the windshield. You probably won't be able to see any of the car behind that.

Rear Three-Quarters Tracking
Level of Difficulty: 4

This shot is harder than the other tracking shots for two reasons: (1) the camera is facing into the wind and vulnerable to any spray, insects, or stones kicked up by either vehicle; (2) the cars need to be closer together, and this can create a problem with shadows or reflections.

When shooting rear tracking, you and the lens are facing forward and vulnerable to bugs and stones thrown up from the road. Be aware of the camera car's shadow creeping into the frame. 35mm 1/60 second f5.6.

Opposite top: When shooting more than one car on a public road you must be very certain that there is nothing coming from the other way, so only do it on closed sections or where you can see clearly on a long, straight stretch. 28mm 1/30 second f8.

Below: Tracking with more than two cars needs to be planned carefully. Set up the positions you want statically so that the drivers know where they should be. Start out slowly in formation and build up speed steadily. 50mm 1/60 second f11

Set up your cars in their static positions with the feature car only a little ahead of the camera car. You want to be shooting about level with the rear of the feature car out of a side window or, even better, the sunroof. This time the feature car will govern the speed the vehicles will be traveling at and the camera car will creep up on the inside to get into the right position.

You should be able to speak to your driver in the camera car to get him exactly where you want him. Again, work out a maneuver to avoid other traffic. This time the feature car should accelerate and the camera car should brake to bring them back into the same lane in the event of an oncoming vehicle.

You'll need to be very careful that you don't get part of the camera car in the shot unless you want to. If you are shooting from one Cobra to another, it sometimes is a good idea to include a bit of the hood or wheel arch in the frame.

If you are shooting into a convertible, make sure the inside of the car is clean and tidy and your driver is not wearing anything too eye-catching that would detract from the car. Also look for a telltale reflection of the camera car in the rear panel of your feature car.

Multiple-Car Tracking
Level of Difficulty: 7

As with the multiple-car panning, this is more difficult due to the increased number of variables involved, but is a great shot to do if you have the time and a suitable location. The racetrack or an old airfield runway is the best place for this as it's too dangerous to get more than two cars alongside on a public road, and few are wide enough anyway.

It's best to shoot out of a sunroof, or kneel in the back of a convertible. You will need a bit of extra height to see all the cars properly and give some depth to your picture. You can shoot a low angle, but the image will end up very long and thin.

Set up your static formation with the camera car in a position in front of the first car in the group. This is okay if you are shooting up to five cars in a line-up, but over that number you will need to consider a second row and a more central position.

Place smaller cars at the front looking over to taller, larger cars at the back of the shot. Work out the triangular view from the camera and place your cars accordingly to fill the frame. Use a wide-angle lens and a shutter speed of 1/125 second.

Start out very slowly, making sure everyone speeds up at the same pace until you reach your shooting speed of about 30 miles per hour. Try to make sure cars overlapas little as possible and balance the shot with the same number

This is a static zoom shot where the car is quite still. In low light conditions with your camera on a low tripod, slide the zoom in or out during a long exposure. 70-200mm zoom 1 second f32.

of cars on each side. The drivers at the front of the shot will be quite close to each other, so make sure they are properly briefed and know what they are doing. Again, the key safety tip for the drivers is not to make any sudden steering moves, or brake or accelerate too fast. Just keep everything slow and smooth.

The cars at the back will need to be proportionally further away so they do not disappear behind the ones at the front. Make sure their drivers can still see you and any signals you may give them to change their speed or move left and right.

Don't forget to let all your drivers know when you are shooting so they don't look at the camera—or appear too terrified!

CORNERING

Level of Difficulty: 7

This is the last of the three main disciplines that you will need to master to complete your portfolio of car photographs and possibly the most difficult. The key problem arises from the high speed of the car coming toward you and the very short time it may be in the frame. Only the very best autofocus lenses will keep the car sharp all the way in, so it's best to learn how to shoot manually.

The idea of the cornering shot is to show how the car handles as it passes through the bend. Body roll, skidding, and under- or oversteer can all be demonstrated in a well-taken cornering shot. Finding the right corner to show all of this isn't that easy because roads today are engineered to make them as safe as possible.

Look for a 90 degree open bend or hairpin curve with good visibility across it and somewhere to get back at least 20 yards. Use a long lens for this shot to

flatten the image and focus only on the car. Anything over a 180mm lens will be fine, but ideally this is the shot for a 300mm.

Choose a quiet road with plenty of light falling on it and avoid corners overhung by trees or in the shade because you may struggle to get a fast enough shutter speed. You'll need 1/500 second or faster to freeze the motion of the car, but leave a bit of movement in the wheels and tires. If you go faster than 1/1000 second there will be no movement in the shot at all and the car may look as though it's parked on the corner, which defeats the purpose of the difficult shot.

Get your driver to drive through the corner a few times and watch to see how the car behaves from different positions on the outside of the bend. This doesn't have to be done at any great speed and depends on how sharp the bend is. Usually a speed of about 30-50 miles per hour will work.

Top: Look for a 90 degree open bend or hairpin curve with good visibility across it and somewhere to get back at least 20 yards. Use a long lens for this shot to flatten the image and focus only on the car. Anything over a 180mm will be fine, but ideally this is the shot for a 300mm. 300mm 1/500 second f4.5. **Above:** Cornering on a loose surface looks great as dust and stones are thrown out by the wheels but be careful—the more dramatic it looks, the more chance there is that the driver might skid off the track altogether. 200mm 1/500 second f8.

Opposite: You have to be lucky to catch an incident at a racetrack. You may only catch one in ten when you are in the right place at the right time. Never turn your back on the direction of traffic and remember to get yourself out of the way if a car is coming toward you. No photograph is worth getting injured for. This D-Type Jaguar ended up ten feet away in an area I had just been moved from by a safety marshal. 300mm 1/500 second f8.

> ### SAFETY
>
> If you are lying by the side of the road, on the outside of a corner, with cars tearing toward you, most folk would say you must be mad. As the saying goes, it certainly helps. Actually this is usually pretty safe due to the long lens you are using and the distance you are from the car.
>
> If your driver does come unstuck and loses it on the bend, the car will travel in the direction of most momentum and should miss you. However, it's a good idea to get a friend to stand behind you and watch the car as it turns the corner. This way, you have someone to yell a warning or haul you out of the way. He can also warn the driver of oncoming traffic.

If you can't find a really tight corner, use a more shallow one and get your driver to turn in hard to accentuate the bend. Newer cars handle much better than classics so you may need to go a bit quicker to show their characteristics.

You will notice that there will be a dead spot where the car no longer appears to be coming toward you, but traveling across in front of the camera. You'll see this best by lying down and getting the camera as low as possible so you can see light coming underneath the car. This is where there will be the maximum roll and potential for lack of traction or even lifting a wheel.

Prefocus on a point two feet in front of where your dead spot is and mark it with a pebble by the side of the road. If you can pick up the car on its way into the corner it will help with your timing. Wait until it reaches a point just before your focusing spot before you squeeze the shutter release. Remember with the high shutter speed that you are likely to be using a wide aperture on all but the brightest days. This means you will need accurate focusing and timing because of the minimal depth of field you will have to work with.

Due to the angle and speed of the car as it advances, you can't wait until it is passing through the focus point before shooting or you will have missed it. A car traveling at 60 miles per hour covers 88 feet in a second, so you must predict where the car is going to be when the shutter actually fires. You won't be able to see the car at that moment as the mirror will be blocking the prism. So if you do see the car sharp for a moment you've probably missed the shot.

You may need to keep practicing this shot for a while before you get the hang of predicting the focus and get some decent results.

ACTION SEQUENCES

Level of Difficulty: 9

Although I mentioned earlier in this section that most autofocus lenses are not quick enough to follow a car through a corner, some are. On a bright day with the light behind you and a plain background beyond, you may be able to follow the car all the way into and out of the corner. This makes for a great sequence of images that run together showing exactly how the car is handling through a bend, or during an incident at an event.

The trick here is that this is a part-cornering, part-panning shot; you will need to move your camera as the car progresses through the sequence. You may find that you can even use your long zoom if you are not too far away, combining three action techniques in one.

Start out with your usual high shutter speed of 1/500 second but try a few slower shot at 1/250 second and 1/125 second, as well. If you get them sharp they will look great with lots of blur in the background and on the road.

As with any of these difficult shots, don't expect to get them perfect the first time. Remember the law of averages says that the more times the car goes past the lens, the better the chances are of getting a great shot.

LANDSCAPE

Level of Difficulty: 4

This is one of the easiest and most effective shots to do in our action section. The reason it has a medium level of difficulty attached to it is for one type of landscape shot only, so don't be put off. This image is of the car, small in the frame, traveling through a spectacular landscape or event. It might be a stunning road through the Rockies or the racetrack and is one of the shots that magazines always want as an establishing shot. Here, the camera is stationary and can be either hand-held or on a tripod.

To stop a car traveling across the frame, you have to use a very fast shutter speed if you want to freeze all motion. It will only be in the right place in the viewfinder for a fraction of a second, so quick reactions are essential. It's a good idea to use a tripod and cable release. Also stand to the side of the camera to give you a much better idea of approaching speed by using both eyes. 50mm 1/2000 second f4.

The key is the location. You are looking for a stunning bit of road in the landscape. It could be a single corner, a series of bends, a vanishing point road, or a road coming in toward, or going diagonally away, from the camera. Try to find a high viewpoint above the road so you look down on it to give it some scale.

The hardest shot of this type is when the road goes across the frame from side to side and you can't govern the speed of the car, e.g., at a race meeting. You will need a very fast shutter speed and reactions to match it, as the car will whiz through the viewfinder in a fraction of a second. Even on a wider lens where you have a second or two to get the shot, if you want to freeze the car you will need to shoot at around 1/2000 second. Due to this high shutter speed, you will only be able to do this shot on bright days with the lens wide open.

All the other variations on this shot are quite straightforward and involve setting a shutter speed of 1/500th or 1/250th second depending on the speed of the car. Prefocus on the section of road where you want the car to be sharp and don't move the camera as the car comes through the frame. Time your run so your feature car is the only one in the frame, as other traffic will distract the eye away from your car.

Shoot just before or at your focus point, as with the cornering shot. Because the car is so small in the frame you don't have to be quite so accurate.

There is a good way to cheat with this shot, place your car exactly where you want it on the road and shoot it standing still. If the car is small enough in the frame, you won't be able to see that the wheels aren't moving and you'll be certain that you've got the shot. Most snappers will shoot both an action version of this shot and a static one just to be safe. Don't forget with the static shot that you will still need your driver in the car and behind the wheel playing the part. Choose a quiet road to stop on and make sure you are not in a dangerous place such as just around a blind bend. By timing when you shoot, you place the car at the exact point in the frame for the greatest impact. You need

With the cars traveling diagonally through the frame you may get more than one opportunity to shoot, so take it. Prefocus on various points in the landscape and practice switching between them when there's nothing to shoot.

300mm 1/350 second f 5.6.

to decide whether you want the car just entering, leaving, or in the middle of the frame. This is where the rule of thirds, one of the laws of composition, can help out. By dividing the frame up into a grid made of imaginary thirds, the eye is drawn to points of interest at the intersecting lines approximately one-third in and one-third up. This means that you don't always put the subject and the horizon in the middle of the frame. Move them a little off-center for greater impact.

IN-CAR ACTION

Level of Difficulty: 4

This is a shot featuring the driver and is taken from inside the car, showing the road and landscape outside the car in a blur. It's most effective in a convertible where you can sit up high on the back seats and see the road ahead. To do this shot you will need your widest lens, flash gun, and steadiest arm.

Do your focusing before you set off, you may not be able to when the car is moving. Choose either the face of the driver or the instrument panel as your focal point, as these are what draw the eye in the cockpit. Don't forget to hold on tight. 24mm 1/30 second f11.

It's best to find a shady road with plenty of background and few or no bumps in it. You'll need trees or buildings in the background to give you the blur; the closer they are to the road, the more blur you will see in the photo.

Take a meter reading outside in the area you will be driving through. The light level shouldn't be too bright, for you don't want to use an aperture of more than about f8 or your flash gun will take too long to recharge.

Shutter speed can be anything from 1/15 second to 1/125 second depending on how fast you go, how much blur you want, and how steady your arm is that day. You may be able to hand-hold right down to 1/15 second if you lean against something in the car, but be careful you are not affected by any engine or road vibration.

The best compromise is about 1/60 second at f8 with the flash set one stop under at f5.6 if the ambient light allows. This should make almost everything in the car sharp and give a good amount of blur outside at 30 miles per hour.

In a four-seat sedan or two-plus-two coupe, climb into the back and poke your lens over the driver's shoulder, looking out the windshield. To see the road you may need to get the camera as high as possible in the cabin, calling for some uncomfortable positions.

Do your focusing before you set off, because you may not be able to when the car is moving. Choose either the face of the driver or the instrument panel as your focal point; as these are what draw the eye in the cockpit.

You don't need to be going any faster than 30 miles per hour to see blur through the windows or on the road, but the faster you do go the more blur you will get. Instruct your driver to accelerate, steer, and brake as smoothly as

possible and not to do anything suddenly. You probably won't be secure in a seat, so you could end up being tossed around inside the interior and hurting yourself or damaging your camera with any sudden car movement.

In addition to shooting over the driver's shoulder, try looking straight across at the driver from the front passenger seat. To do this, you will need to lean against the passenger door so make sure it is properly shut and locked. Use your widest lens (20-28 mm and 1/30 second) and fill-in flash. Again, this is easier in a convertible because you can sit on the edge of the door with the window all the way down. Don't forget to secure yourself by hooking your feet under the front seat or get a friend to hold onto your legs.

Another great angle is to lie down in the front passenger footwell and look up at the driver. You'll get a great view past the gearshift and from behind the steering wheel. You'll need fill-in flash set at 1/2 stop under or even 1/1 to correctly light your driver against the bright background of the sky or overhanging trees.

This shot can be done as static. Park up in an area with no background but the sky. Try to shoot in the morning or evening before there is any direct sunlight or on a

Set the camera flash to one stop under the outside reading. If the car has a pale-colored roof lining you can bounce the flash to soften it on the driver's face. 20-35mm 1/30 second f5.6.

Shooting part of the car on the move works well as a graphic detail and an action shot.

28mm f16 1 second

cloudy day to avoid problems with contrast. Open the car door and kneel on the ground, getting as low as you can into the footwell so you are looking up at the driver. Make sure he has his hands on the wheel or gearshift and eyes on the road ahead. It's a good idea to set up as though the driver is turning in toward the photographer. This way you will see more of the driver's face, as he leans into the corner, giving the shot more of an action feel. It's important that you don't have anything visible in the background, as this is where you would see blur if you were moving.

The last of these in-car shots doesn't involve the driver at all. It's a view of a part of the car moving in the landscape. A good example is looking forward over the windshield from a convertible to the road ahead, or try leaning out of the rear window and shooting the tail of the car with the road snaking away behind. For this shot choose a very smooth road. Find a road with a few turns for a good view of the road going away. Shoot at anything from 1/125-1/30 second, depending on light conditions and the amount of blur required. Be careful not to lean directly on the body if you are shooting at speed. If the car hits a bump, you may dent it or your camera.

You can also get a great shot of the front wheel blurred against the road by leaning out of the front passenger window while the car is turning tight circles. Shoot at 1/30 second with plenty of space around and don't forget to lock the door you are leaning on.

Try using your flash gun and a really slow shutter speed for a flash and blur shot. Go for 1/8-1/2 second and set the flash at 1/1 with the ambient outside meter reading and shoot in the evening or on a heavily shaded road so you don't have to wait too long for your flash gun to recharge. Hand-hold the camera using your widest lens and don't worry too much about camera shake, as the flash will freeze the foreground.

Yomping

Level of Difficulty: 7

This shot got its name from the way the Scandinavian rally drivers used to talk of jumping the car over bumps in the road at speed. Its level of difficulty depends on the speed of the jump and the angle of the shot.

Shutter speed depends on the speed of the cars. For fast cars coming toward you on a rally stage, you will need a very high shutter speed of about 1/2000 second to freeze them in the air and lots of light or a very fast film. But you can shoot much slower if your subject is traveling slower, or you pan the car in the air. Try coming down to 1/250 second and prefocus carefully on the spot where you are going to shoot. Choose the spot by watching a few cars go through and noting where they are at their highest off the road.

Make sure you are shooting from a safe place, because once the car has taken off, the driver can do nothing to steer it. Check with the event marshals if you are not sure.

This is a good shot to use at off-road events such as mud-plugging, trialing, or hill-climbs, where the speed of the car may be only a few miles an hour. Watch each section and look for places where the car pops out of a hole or over a steep edge, getting some "air" or lifting its front wheels. A lower angle on this shot will make the "yomp" appear higher in the photo.

Prefocus on the spot where the car will be at the apex of its jump and pan it into shooting position if you can see it approaching. If you are using a motordrive, shoot a burst of three frames so you have a sequence to choose from.

200mm 1/500 second f8.

BOLT-ON GOODIES AND SPECIAL EQUIPMENT

Level of Difficulty: 6

This section is all about gadgets you can attach to the camera, or attach the camera to, for a special effect. Some of them are expensive and some you can make yourself, adapting tools from other applications. Many of the items mentioned here are not necessarily made for cameras, and you may have to look through professional lighting catalogs or camera grip websites to find them. "Grip" covers all

This suction device will stick to anything smooth and flat. With a lightweight camera mounted on the top, you pump the air out to attach it. The pump must be checked regularly because it does lose its suction quite quickly.

Shot using the suction cup on a smooth, quiet road with the engine switched off to avoid any vibration. The photographer is pushing the car at around 1 mile per hour while pressing the shutter release. Note the dials at zero and ignition light. 20mm 2 seconds f16.

Opposite: Attaching your camera to a moving car is usually reserved for the movie grip technician, but a few accessory companies have come up with some useful gadgets that can be used for stills cameras. The technique is somewhat different for stills cameras; most gadget shots are done at very low speeds using long shutter speeds. 28mm 2 seconds f22.

Shooting from the side is possible with this window mounting. To avoid any movement in the glass and to keep the camera steady, roll the window down until there is only about three inches of the glass still exposed. A pop of flash can be a good idea set at one or two stops under the ambient exposure.

the equipment used to fix a camera to anything from a tripod to a moving airplane.

Attaching a camera to a moving car is a task usually reserved for the professional movie grip technician, but a few accessory companies have come up with some useful gadgets that can be used for still cameras. The technique is somewhat different for still cameras, as most gadget shots are done at very low vehicle speeds using long shutter speeds.

STILL PHOTOGRAPHS

Level of Difficulty: 3

When using a long exposure, it is important that you don't jog the camera when you press the shutter. You can use an ordinary cable release but a far better system clips onto the hot shoe of your camera and fires the shutter by remote control. This is a wireless trigger that costs about $400 and is available for most top of the range cameras. It will work from up to 200 yards away or further with a straight line of view. It can also be used to great effect in a race car on the track where the camera is attached to the roll bar and the driver doesn't have the time to fire the shutter himself. You can set it for single or multiple firings and connect it up to more than one camera with the remote by using different channels. Make sure you have fresh batteries each time you want to use both the trigger and the remote; you don't want to discover it hasn't worked and you've missed the shot after the event.

The most useful piece of grip equipment is the "Super Clamp"—a chunky metal clamp that attaches to other grip items with a universal sized spigot. This is useful for attaching cameras straight onto the roll bar of a car or in conjunction with other clamps and poles to make a "short rig" to shoot the car while moving.

The short rig is a simplified form of the boom or big rig system used by advertising photographers. The latter systems cost thousands of dollars to make or hire and require a number of specialists to operate.

By using the short rig you will be able to safely shoot a part of the car with maximum blur, in a relatively short amount of time, with the minimum of cash outlay. An A-frame short rig is the most complex of these, allowing the camera to be fitted out away from the car by about two yards.

You will need:

- Three Super Clamps and six spigots.
- Two telescopic lightweight poles (painters often use for painting high ceilings, so try your DIY store).
- A camera clamp to fit the base of your camera.
- A long adjustable luggage strap with a tensioner.

Other useful items are:

- A suction cup with a Super Clamp fitting.
- A few other clamps of various sizes.
- Some soft cloths to protect body panels.
- Extra luggage straps.

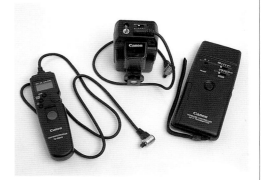

This is a wireless trigger and is available for most top-range cameras. It costs about $400. It will work from up to 200 yards away or further with a straight line of view. The remote on the right is a timer that will set off the shutter at regular intervals.

You will need to decide if you want to shoot the front or the rear of the car. If it has a low air dam at the front, the back may be better as it will be difficult to get the clamps and poles under it. Choose a quiet, smooth flat road, because it may take up to an hour to set up your shot. Have a good background to give you the blur.

Attach the clamps to the underside of the car with the spigot holes facing out backward at a converging angle. You may need two—one on each side of the car—or only one if you plan to use the suction cup as well. Hammer the spigots into the end of your long poles and fit them into the Super Clamps under the car so you have a basic A-shape out the back and to one side of the car. Fix the A at the apex with another clamp and attach your camera fixing to the top.

Wrap your adjustable luggage strap around the Super Clamp at the apex and attach the other end to the far side of the trunk lid or to a point inside the car through the opposite side window. Take up the tension using the adjuster until the A-frame lifts off the road. It will need to be at least a couple of inches off the road surface to work properly. If the strap adjuster is metal, be careful to pad it so that it does-n't rub on the paintwork. You may need to play around using different clamps, poles, or suckers to get the camera just right, as fitting requirements will be different for every car.

Set the camera up with a wide angle pointing down the rear three-quarters side of the car, making sure none of your rig is in the shot or reflected into the side of the car. Have plenty of background in the frame.

The driver must sit absolutely still for this long exposure. Again, it's best done with the engine off and a gentle shove by the photographer or a helper to get the car moving. 20mm 4 seconds f22.

Take your ambient light reading allowing for the fact that it will need to be at least one second to work—but five seconds will be better. Evening or early morning is ideal, but if it's a bit bright you could try a Neutral Density (ND) filter in front of the lens.

Make sure the engine is switched off and your driver is in position behind the wheel. Move the car back a few yards and start it moving with a smooth push at about a half-mile per hour. It will help if you can get a friend to push for you so you can concentrate on operating the camera. As it gets to your shooting spot, fire the shutter with a cable release or remote trigger and keep pushing at a steady pace.

Repeat the whole exercise trying different shutter speeds. Depending on the light, you should be able to go all the way down to 30 seconds if your pushing and the road are smooth enough.

A simpler, small rig involves the sucker apparatus you can buy with the camera fitting on top. This is good on its own on a flat trunk lid or stabilized with another short pole on the side of a car. When using the sucker, frequently check that it is secure and not losing its suction.

You can make a basic periscope viewfinder to allow you to get the camera as low as possible when you are shooting car-to-car pictures. (You could also buy a short periscope viewfinder, but they are very expensive and not long enough.) Use your existing eyecup holder that slots onto the back of your SLR's viewfinder or buy a new one. Salvage the inside of a paper towel roll and cut a flap into the bottom. Onto this, glue a small piece of mirror about one inch square. Your local glasscutter will probably give you the mirror and may even cut it to size for you. Tape the camera eyepiece to the bottom of the card board tube, level with the mirror, so when you look down from the top you can see through the viewfinder.

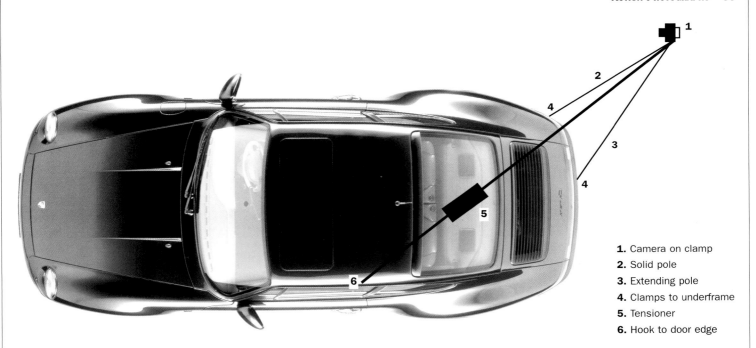

1. Camera on clamp
2. Solid pole
3. Extending pole
4. Clamps to underframe
5. Tensioner
6. Hook to door edge

It's a bit fussy to get the angle just right, but when you do you should be able to hold the camera ten inches lower and still see what's going on. Remember, because you're using a mirror, the image will be upside down and flipped, but it should be okay for basic framing solutions, such as making sure the car is it the correct position in the viewfinder.

REVIEW

- **Safety must come first.**
- **Choose the right shutter speed for the image.**
- **Watch for the decisive moment.**
- **Use walkie-talkies if you have them.**
- **Find the right location with a simple background.**
- **Don't ask your drivers to do anything they are not confident about.**
- **Use seatbelts or a safety harness if available.**
- **Don't break any laws to get your photos.**

If you have time, set up for a mini-rig shot. You'll need about an hour to get all your clamps and poles in position, so plan it for the end of the day. To avoid any vibration during the very long exposure or damage to the car, make sure that none of your poles rub on the bodywork. 28mm 4 seconds f22.

Chapter 5
Motorsport Events

Try to get an establishing shot that shows the setting for the track. If you're shooting for a magazine this is the type of picture that might be selected as a lead image. 35mm 1/125 second f11.

One of the places where you can get some great photographs is at the racetrack. Using the techniques shown in the earlier sections, there's plenty of opportunity for practicing your action photography. This chapter will show you how to safely and efficiently get the most out of this exciting situation.

Unless you are a well-known photographer it is sometimes difficult to get a trackside pass at major events but at smaller ones you may get one if you contact the organizers a few weeks beforehand.

If you can't get a track pass there are still plenty of places to get great shots.

PLANNING YOUR RACE

Knowing your subject is half the battle in shooting great pictures at the racetrack. If you know which cars are the fastest, the famous drivers, and your way around the track, it will make it much easier to get the photographs you want.

The key is to plan your race day so you have a good spread of different shots featuring all the star cars, celebrated drivers and winners, as well as some atmosphere photographs.

First, get hold of a program and spend some time going through the races to mark the cars and drivers that you want to shoot. If you don't know the circuit, look at the map and work out where there might be opportunities for taking pictures. Look to see if there are driver signings scheduled into the day. These are great opportunities to get portraits of famous drivers in a good mood. If there are action photos from past meetings in the program determine where they were taken. Program photos are often a good guide to the best angles at a track you don't know.

If you get time, walk around the circuit and take a look at the good corners from the inside and outside and at the grid, working out the quickest way to get to each. Talk to other photographers who know the track and ask them for ideas. Remember the track may be open for you to cross or walk on before the races get going, but it usually closes at least 15 minutes before each race.

Take a walk around the paddock and talk to the drivers or their teams to find out any inside information you can about who might win or what their race strategy is going to be. Keep your eyes open for possible photos here as you may spot well-known drivers or see cars being worked on or other interesting images. This is a great place for getting really close to the cars and shooting details, but don't get in the way and remember to ask permission. A team member who sees you shooting in a professional way may even ask you to shoot some pictures for them out on the track.

If you do get talking to a team in the paddock before the race, ask if you could put a camera in the car for pictures during the race. You'll need a wireless trigger and a separate flash gun connected by a cable to the camera because the remote receiver goes onto the hot shoe. You'll also have to face the reality of what might happen to your camera if your driver has a nasty accident.

For many races, if you want to go trackside you'll need a special pass. These are difficult to get for big events, but are often available at smaller meetings if you contact the organizers a few weeks before. 28mm 1/60 second f16.

The start is often the most exciting part of a race, so get yourself in a good position. There will nearly always be a warm-up lap for you to run through your shots. 200mm 1/500 second f5.6.

Make sure that you test the equipment before the start and that your driver is willing to have a flash gun go off in the cockpit. Get in a position where other cars will be close by, such as on a chicane with a clear view of the track. Use the remote only at the start or when you see your driver is having a battle with someone, or the pictures will be a bit dull after the first few frames' novelty has worn off.

Also go to the pits before the races start, and check the program to see if any races have driver changes, which will happen there. This is usually a very exciting part of the race, with drivers climbing in and out of the cars as quickly as they can, refueling or changing tires before tearing back out onto the track to rejoin the race. If you've planned to shoot the driver change or pit stop don't forget to be in position with time to spare.

When you have a trackside pass, work out where you are going to be for each race. Speak to the marshals and check that it will be safe to be there during the race, make sure you show them the correct passes and follow their safety advice.

Before the start and at the end of each race, the cars will very often be directed into a holding area. This can be a good place to get some in-car portraits of the drivers if you have the right passes. But be careful, as drivers can be a bit prickly just before they go out to risk their lives on the racetrack!

If there are famous cars or drivers, give yourself an extra chance for some great shots and shoot them during the practice sessions. Go for single-car panning or cornering shots and make sure not to include other cars, so no one will know that the photo wasn't taken during the race.

Try some really slow pans at 1/8 second during practice, or other arty shots that you wouldn't risk shooting during the race, and decide which positions around the track are the best for photographing the race itself. Ideally you should choose your locations so that you can shoot more than one angle from them. Your first may be of the grid with a wide angle, your second as they come around again with a telephoto onto the start/finish straight, and maybe a panning shot as they pass on the third lap.

TOP TIP

Don't shoot until you see the whites of their eyes! Set up your prefocused shots carefully and wait for the cars to pass through your focal point. Don't be tempted to refocus as they move into the frame.

Plan to be in the best position for the start of each race. Overlooking the grid and at the first corner are very good spots. You will always gets lots of action as they tear away from the line and vie for position into turn one. This can be either a long tele-photo shot or a wide shot and is a good one to use as an establishing opener in your set of photographs of the race meeting.

Listen to the commentary both before and during the race. Mark any last minute driver changes into your program to prevent making mistakes later. Keep track of

The first corner on the first lap with drivers jockeying for their places is another great place to be at the start of a race. Pre-focus carefully and keep shooting after the front cars have gone through as there is often a tangle of car further down the grid. 300 mm 1/500 second f4.

SAFETY

Make sure you stop shooting and get out of the way if it looks like the cars involved or bits of them might be coming your way. Quite a few photographers and marshals have been killed at race tracks by not paying full attention, or facing the wrong direction at the scene of an accident.

Above left: Watch for racing battles between drivers. Overtaking maneuvers make for great panning opportunities. Keep your focus on one car and the other will blur as its speed changes. 180mm 1/30 second f11.

If you see a car lift a wheel at a corner get ready for the next time it comes around because it'll probably happen again. Try to shoot groups of cars tussling for position—it makes for much more exciting pictures than cars on their own. 300mm 1/500 second f4.5

who is winning or having a good drive and make sure you've got a couple of frames of them before the end of the race.

After the start try to shoot only groups of cars and the winners. This way you won't have lots of pictures with vast amounts of track and only one car looking lost. Remember, in race photography, composition is more a matter of knowing when not to shoot.

It's now time to move to your next position for the rest of the race. Make sure it's not too far away so you don't get there and find the race is over. Pack up your camera gear as fast as you can and walk quickly to the new spot. Try to ignore the fact that the race is going on around you. You may miss a few laps, but should be in position in to shoot the winners as they go past a couple of times at the end of the race.

As circuits get safer, photographers are pushed further away behind gravel traps, so go for the tight slower curves where you can get close to the edge of the track and won't need a 500mm lens.

In local club racing, most races last only about ten laps so you may only have 15-20 minutes of actual race time to shoot in. Longer races should allow you to get around to all the best places if it's not too crowded, but try to shoot as much as you can at the start before the cars get too strung out.

Sometimes you'll encounter a gap in the racing for lunch or a race that doesn't interest you. Try using that time to get out to a shooting position on the far side of the track that no one else may have been to. Shoot the start as usual but then head back ASAP so you don't get stuck out there for too long and miss the next race.

If you own or have hired a long lens for the race, try some shots looking down the long straightaways in addition to your cornering images. This is a good start shot with lots of cars dotting the track, but it is surprisingly difficult if they are going really quick so you'll need a high shutter speed (1/1000 second), and a carefully pre-focused lens. It's a good idea to use a monopod with a long lens at the racetrack, as they can be very heavy and difficult to hold level.

All the excitement might not be going on at the front; look for racing battles going on further down the grid and get a few frames of them as they go by on different laps. There may be some excellent chances for multiple-car panning as cars pass each other on the straightaways. These are best shot from high up in the grandstand to give yourself plenty of space and the chance to see all the cars involved.

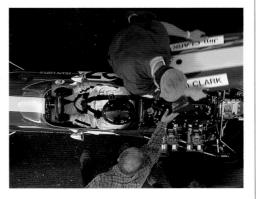

If the race has a pit stop or a driver change, get to the pits a lap or two before to be ready when they start coming in. Remember to keep out of the way of the pit crews, as they will be working against the clock. 50mm 1/30 second f8.

Don't forget the behind-the-scenes action in the paddock. There's plenty of opportunity for getting some great shots here, particularly before each race as teams get ready to go onto the track. 35mm 1/125 second f11.

Keep your eyes open for celebrities around the circuit. Driver signings are a good place for getting close and for getting a picture or two. Don't forget to ask before you stick your camera into anyone's face. Stirling Moss in the 300SLR. 24mm 1/125 second f5.6.

On tight corners, if you can get low enough, you may find that some cars will lift a wheel or lose grip and slide as they turn in. Remember which cars are doing it and be ready next time they come around. For normal cornering, use shutter speeds of 1/500 second or above for really fast corners and cars.

Look out for accidents or racing incidents; they often make for great pictures. These are often grab shots, so it helps if you have autofocus and are pointing in the right direction when it happens.

Don't shoot after an accident if you can see that someone might have been hurt—as you won't be very popular with the organizers or relatives of the injured person.

Be careful what you line up in the background of your pictures. Avoid busy billboards or crowds close to the track when shooting a cornering shot, because the car can easily disappear into them. These make better backgrounds for panning, as they are colorful and will be blurred in the final image.

Remember, if you can't get close enough with your telephoto lens, make sure the image is as sharp as possible so you can blow it up and crop it into the frame later.

It makes a big difference to the composition as to where the car is in the frame and you may not be able to control this as much as you like at the track. Cropping the image on allows you to think about it more so you can place the car exactly where you want in the final picture.

Ration yourself to a set number of films or exposures per race so you don't overshoot but make sure you keep one spare roll for that surprise right at the end of the day. Shoot some images of characters in the crowd or of the race mechanics to add a little color and variety.

If you are close to the podium at the end of the race, get a few shots of the winners as they are given their trophies, but don't forget to allow yourself enough time to get in position again for the start of the next race, if there is one.

Choose your shutter speed carefully on a rally. You need to make every shot count, because you won't get a second chance. Try to pick a section of road where you can get a few different angles, maybe even of each car as it comes toward you, passes, and goes away. There will probably be a few minutes between each car so you should have time to move around a little at each place. 50mm 1/250 second f11.

Many rally photographers use print film or digital as it offers higher shutter speeds in gloomy conditions. Check ahead on your rally maps for suitable locations and be ready to move on to the next after a few cars have passed by. 300mm 1/500 second f2.8.

SAFETY

Never stand on the outside of a corner without something very solid in front of you.

SAFETY

Remember you will be driving on the same difficult roads, possibly in treacherous conditions without the benefit of a rally car or the skills to control it, so take it easy. Don't break the speed limit and always err on the side of caution.

ON A RALLY

There are many different types of rally events, from historic to modern and stage to navigation, and a lot of the track racing photography principles are the same.

A good plan is essential, and knowing the cars and the locations is a great bonus. The main problems you may encounter are the great distances covered during a day, the isolation of some stages, and the low light conditions you may find when you get there.

A stage rally blasts along a section of road or track over anything from a mile up to 50 miles. The cars go individually, trying to go as fast as they can to cover the distance in the shortest time.

The roads are often very poor, sometimes remote, and the rallies may be held when conditions are particularly bad to make them more challenging. But it is possible to hike in to photograph them with a good set of maps and the right equipment.

Ideally, you need to get the same maps as the rally teams themselves and go over them to find a point that is accessible to a nearby open road. You should be able to find out which maps you need from the organizers weeks before, although the actual route may be secret until a few days before the event. Get there early and stake your position at a good location on the inside of a corner or at a water splash. There may be marshals on the section but if you are away from the start or finish there may be none, so be very careful where you stand. Watch a few cars go through and adjust your position to the optimum.

If you are in a forest and it's a bit dark, choose a fast film or up-rate your next roll, not forgetting to mark what ASA you have shot it at.

One of the most effective shots is to use fill-in flash on a medium telephoto lens (80-135mm) and pan the car as it goes by. Try to choose an open panning spot with a good view down the track to get as much warning as possible of when the car is coming.

Another approach that works well is to frame a spectacular landscape with the rally road going through it.

Stage rallies complete one section and then move on to the next, rarely doing more than two stages in any one day. You should have time to get back to your car and be in position for the start of the next section in plenty of time as long as you don't wait to see the tail enders.

Navigation rallies often run over long distances and are designed around tortuous routes. Because the cars may have to adhere to a strict average speed over the section, navigation rallies are not usually high-speed events. Yet, some cars try to make up time in between and really go for it.

Unless you know the country or have knowledge of good locations for photography, the best way to cover a navigation rally is to drive the route along with the competitors to find good spots. Because they are usually open-road events, you'll need a good driver and the same maps as the rally cars, although sections of the route may be marked along the way. Look at the list of entrants to see how many there are, who you are interested in, and where they are in the running order. Study the map for likely shooting locations, such as bridges or mountain passes, and mark them as possible stop-off points.

Park your car down the road from the start if you need to shoot it or follow the route ahead of all the cars until you see a location you like. Get the car well off the road and out of danger before you set up for your picture and wait. After the first five or so have gone through, jump back into the car and move on to your next spot. Be very careful as you pull back onto the road to not balk any following competitors. If a rally car comes up behind you, pull over at the first opportunity and let it pass.

At the next location, shoot another five cars before moving on and continue to do this throughout the day or until there are no more cars left. This is a good general plan for shooting this type of rally but there are certain problems with it. You may miss the cars you want driving between your locations and not all the locations you will find will be as good.

The other approach is to drive the route as far ahead of the rally cars as you can—maybe even the previous day—and check out the best position. Then only take shots at this position. You will be sure to get a great photo of each car but your pictures will lack the variety of the other system.

Toward the end of the last day make sure you quit the route early enough to make it down to the finish for the presentations and the party.

Don't forget the start and the finish on a rally, which is often quite a party and much more accessible than the racing scene. The start and finish are good places to get portraits of the drivers and co-drivers. 35mm 1/125 second f8.

There are many other types of local motoring events going on most weekends that you won't need any kind of pass to shoot at with lots of potential for great action pictures.
200mm 1/250 second f4.5.

HILLCLIMBS, SPRINTS, AND OFF-ROAD

Some of the oldest events in motorsport aren't track based at all and still run today. They are run on short sections of road and timed individually against the clock. Others shoot up impossibly steep hills with hairpin curves or twist through woodlands between narrow gates and are designed to test the skill of the driver as well as the competence of the car.

The great thing about these events is that they will be open to all photographers and you won't need any special equipment to get great pictures. Although for some of the speed events, you may need to contact the organizers beforehand to get a photographer's pass. The marshals will expect you to be responsible your own safety and you will probably be allowed to get as close to the competing cars as you like.

As with the other races and rallies, it is best to find out as much event information as you can ahead of time. You need to know the route, speed, names, and numbers of the competitors, so buy a program and read it through. Then walk the course and work out the best locations.

If the event is on grass, be very careful not to get into dangerous positions where you may get squashed by cars sliding down hills or off the outside of corners. Big four-wheel drive vehicles may only be crawling over the landscape, but they can still get into trouble and lose control at very low speeds.

Use your wide-angle lens close up from a low vantage point to get spectacular pictures of cars leaping off the top of a steep hillclimb, or longer lenses to capture off-roaders wading through a river. The competitors and spectators at these events are among the friendliest you'll find, so get to know them and take their photos—even if they're all covered in mud.

Shooting in a crowd is hard, so try to get some height and an overview of the whole event. Look for a well-placed window in a nearby building or a hill to give you the elevation. 70mm 1/125 second f11.

Borrow a step ladder to give you height amongst the cars, but be very careful not to damage any cars when you are setting up and moving around. You can get some unusual angles from high up, so shoot some details as well as wide-angle views.

Opposite left: If you can't go up, consider other ideas for creating that different image. If you do use a wide-angle lens close up make sure you have the camera and any visible horizon level. 35mm 1/60 second f11.

Opposite right: An outrageous wheelie car is accelerating. Use a fast panning speed to be sure of getting it sharp and give the background a little blur. 180mm f5.6 1/25th sec.

Keep an eye out for the judges at concours events as they go around examining the cars. It can make for some good people pictures. The owners try to impress the judges and show their car off to its best potential. 28mm 1/125 second f8.

Keep your eyes open for local events. There may be banger racing, trailing, mud-plugging, kart racing, stock cars, demolition derby, sand racing, autocross, rallycross, as well as vintage and historic club meetings—all of which should give you plenty to get involved in.

REVIEW

- **Plan your race carefully.**
- **Walk the course beforehand if you can.**
- **Know when not to shoot.**
- **Ration your film so you don't overshoot and run out.**
- **Shoot groups of cars; they look more interesting.**
- **If you don't own one, why not hire a long lens?**
- **Watch out for racing battles further down the grid.**
- **Get a full set of rally maps from the organizers.**
- **Take a driver when following a rally.**

SHOWS

Some of the most common places to get close to exotic cars is at a show, auction preview, or a car museum. Unfortunately, these are among the worst places to photograph them-parked on grass if outside, crowded in on themselves, or inside under spotlights. Yet there are ways of coming away with great shots if you take your pictures with care.

Outside

Most car shows take place outside in the summer where hundreds of cars will jam onto a large area of grass or a superstore parking lot—not very rich pickings if you want to get that perfect shot of a car you love.

You'll need all your charm and cunning, with a bit of amateur psychology and some luck to pull it off.

If you do find a great car you want to shoot, but it's crammed onto some corner or crowded in with a bunch of tatty old jalopies, find the owner and ask

if you can take a picture of him with it. He's bound to say yes. Wander around the car trying to get a good angle for a few minutes and then go back and explain that you can't get a clean shot because of all the other cars, trees, and trash cans all around it. Ask politely if it would be possible to move it to a better spot.

Now, this is where you need to know a little about how car shows work...

Many owners will bring their cars to shows for one thing only—prizes and awards. They can get very competitive about it, although they won't admit it. Restoration companies will be able to charge top dollar if they have show winners in their stable. There may be cups for Best Restored Car, Best Original Car, Best Car Club, etc., and finally, "Best in Show."

Before the cars are judged, the owners will be busy buffing the paint work, blacking the tires, and generally fussing over their pride and joy. This is not a good time to try for your picture. Have a look around the immediate vicinity for a location you like with good access and think about what pictures you will take. Bide your time until after the judging but before they announce the awards. This way the owner will be happy and relaxed with time on his hands and is more likely to say yes when you ask about moving the car.

Burn out at Goodwood. This Camaro is picking up speed fast. Use a high shutter speed pan to be sure both car and background are sharp. 170mm f5.6 1/500th sec.

Top: Look for interesting angles of view and selectively crop to draw in your subject and isolate it from its surroundings. 180mm f8 180th sec.
Above: Use the location to the full at a show. This one was amongst shiny skyscrapers. 50mm f11 1/125th sec and fill-in flash.

Be as quick as you can, but don't rush. First take a shot of the owner with the car. Then inquire if you can get a few shots of the car on its own and ask how long you can have with the car so you can plan your pictures. Remember to ask for the owners' address so you can send along a copy of the photo—you may meet them again at the next show with a different car you want to shoot and they will be much more pleased to see you if they got their photo.

If they say no to moving the car, you'll have to be even more creative to get a good shot but there are still plenty of opportunities. Look around to see if anyone has a stepladder and ask if you can borrow it for a few minutes. If you can't find one, see if there's a nearby hotel or store that might lend you one. You may have to leave a deposit but it will get you out of a hole and is definitely worth the effort. Be careful when shooting from a set of steps on a wide angle that you don't get the bottom of the ladder in the frame. Also, watch out for those dreaded reflections; Try to minimize them by hanging your coat or a cloth over the ladder.

If you can't find a ladder anywhere ask yourself, "Is there any other way of gaining some height to shoot from?" I've shot from windows, roofs, on top of a truck, speaker stands, trees, and even a pallet on a fork-lift truck. Make sure wherever you go you have permission and it's safe. There are only two rules to remember—don't fall off and don't drop your camera on the car!

If you can't find anything to get you that bit of height, don't give up. Try going the other way. Lie on the ground and look up at the car, zoom in, and just shoot a detail or bite your lip and move on to the next car. It's far better to come home with a dozen shots you are pleased with than 50 you aren't.

Inside

Quite a lot of shows, including the main national shows, may be inside. Most museums and car shows also display their cars indoors. The main pitfall here is the appalling lighting. Stands are rigged with colored spotlights that bounce off the paint in thousands of tiny highlights that do nothing to show off the shape of the car. Fluorescent lighting may mix with daylight in museums, and auctions are often held in semi-opaque tents. Despite the poor lighting, these venues are great places to see the manufacturers' new concept cars, rare racers, or celebrities' cars up close.

The best way to get good photos in these settings is to shoot with the camera on a tripod using a long exposure and a pop of flash to fill in the foreground. If you set your flash gun to fire at one stop under the ambient light reading it will neutralize any weird colors from the spotlights or other artificial lamps.

A typical exposure on a 35mm lens would be f8 at 1 second with the flash filling in at f5.6, but experiment to see what works best. Remember, the rules about a light or

Getting some height to change your angle of view will make for a much more interesting image. This is shot through a window on a wide aperture to be sure that any dirt or reflections from it are not sharp.

The evening light on these race cars at a show really brings out the colors and using a long lens squashes them together in the frame. 180mm f5.6 1/125th second

At indoor shows where you are unsure of the type of artificial lighting, use your camera on a tripod and give a long exposure with a pop of flash one stop under the aperture setting to neutralize any color problems in the foreground.
35mm 1 second f8.

dark subject still apply so open up on the TTL light reading for a dark car and stop down for a light-colored car.

The big national and international car shows often put cars on fantastic sets that give great opportunities for exciting angles that you would get nowhere else. They also place cars on rotating plinths, which can be a problem if you need a long exposure becasue the car will disappear into the background. Ask nicely and they will usually stop the car at the angle you want to get your photo, but be quick.

REVIEW

■ *Choose the right moment to ask owners for permission to shoot their car.*

■ *Get some height to change your angle of view.*

■ *Use fill-in flash and a tripod inside.*

■ *If you use a wide lens close up, make sure the camera is level.*

■ *Ask people politely to move if they are in the way.*

If there is any visible daylight, use it when shooting at an indoor show. Fix the camera on a tripod and use a long exposure with a pop of fill-in flash at one stop under the metered reading to neutralize any other lighting.

Chapter 6
Groups of Cars

Photographing large groups of cars is a minefield. It's like fitting a jigsaw puzzle together without a picture to guide you. The problems are that it is very easy to lose one car behind another, create color patterns that distract the eye, and run out of space at your location. Combine this with organizing a large group of owners who all want their pride and joy to be at the front and you've got quite a headache.

Pairs of cars present little problem except location. These Corvettes were shot in an iron ore depot at the docks after we'd given up all hope of finding a location at the end of a long day. 70mm 1/8 second f22.

The key here is confidence. It's almost impossible to plan exactly where you want each car to go beforehand, so you will have to slot them in as you go and see what looks right. If you waiver making a decision about the angle and positioning of the cars, people will start popping up all over the place with unwanted advice. Pick one or two assistants to aid you with moving cars into position and communicate all your directions through them.

For larger groups, getting a higher camera view-point is essential. Place larger or lighter -olored cars toward the middle or back of the frame so they draw the eye into the image and don't distract by being too prominent at the front. 35mm 1/30 second f11.

Use depth of field and a telephoto lens to flatten the perspective and draw the cars together. The cars will need to be further apart so make sure your camera is on a tripod as you may need to use a long exposure. 135mm 1/2 second f22.

Choosing your location and camera position are very important. If you are shooting a large group (over six cars), you will probably need to gain some height to fit all of them into the frame. Although it's tempting, don't use a really wide-angle lens close up to squeeze everyone in unless you absolutely have to. The cars in the foreground will appear much bigger in the frame than the ones at the back. If you only have a small location, and have to use a wide lens, avoid placing cars toward the edge of the frame because they may look distorted in the picture.

With a standard or mid-telephoto lens, your camera position may be quite a distance away from the cars. This is why you have the assistants who can relay your instructions via walkie-talkie or directly to each driver so you won't lose your voice yelling to them.

You will always need more space than you think. After you get five or six cars in the frame and

you've got another 12 to get in the picture, you'll wonder where all that parking lot space went.

If you have time, mark the triangular frame of the angle of view on the ground with pieces of tape. This will help your assistants to place the cars within the camera's viewfinder, and if you are short-handed, it allows you to come down from the camera to assist them moving cars around without the worry of cropping anything out. Don't forget to remove the pieces of tape before you shoot.

Start at the front of the frame nearest the camera and put the smallest car or any convertibles you have pointing into the center of the frame. Try to avoid putting white or light-color cars at the very front becasue they will stop the eye in the final photograph.

Choose a location with lots of space to spare so you can expand into it if you need to. Good examples of these are hard sand beaches, racetracks, or clean parking lots without white lines. We could have done with a bit more height for this shot of Carroll Shelby at Laguna Seca. 180mm 1/125 second f11.

Continue bringing cars up into the remaining space and not to overlap the fronts or distinctive features of any individual car. Be aware that your picture will look better if you spread same colored cars throughout the frame and don't bunch them up in one area, as that may become a distraction. Finish up with the tallest or longest car at the back. It's sometimes a good idea to park this last car horizontally to make up a little for its reduction in size due to perspective.

Take one final look over the group before you shoot to make sure all the cars look their best. Wheels shoudl be turned slightly away from camera or straight, doors and hoods need to be fully closed, antennae down, sun visors level with the windshield, slipcovers over convertibles tops, etc. Also, watch out for people or stray dogs wandering around in the background or trash blowing into the frame.

When all is looking good, shoot your film as quickly as possible so that none of the elements out of your control change before you get your chance.

Photographs with two, three, or four cars in them are fine shot from normal tripod height. Although if there is an opportunity to shoot from a window or some tall steps, check that out becasue it will probably make for a more interesting

If there's time, why not ask all the owners into the picture at the end for one big group shot? Place them behind the first row of cars so they don't block out too many of the cars behind. 50mm 1/15 second f16.

final image. As before, it's a good idea to crop the nearest car somewhere around the windsheild when using a less than standard lens to even up the sizes of the cars in the picture.

Pairs of cars are straightforward compared to groups and will allow you a much broader choice of options. Try nose-to-nose from side-on, in a "V" formation pointing at the camera, or front three-quarters view and rear three-quarters view together.

Opposite: As you assemble the group, you will need to constantly check through the viewfinder to make sure the cars are how you want them. You can crop into the nearer ones leaving their tails out of the picture; this will give you greater flexibility regarding where you put the cars behind them. 70mm 1/60 second f11.

REVIEW

- ■ *Choose a location with more space than you need.*
- ■ *Gain some height.*
- ■ *Appoint a couple of assistants.*
- ■ *Place smaller cars at the front.*
- ■ *Don't place white cars cl the camera.*

REMEMBER

When you come to shoot, don't forget you will need a large depth of field to be sure all the cars are in focus, so choose a small aperture. This may leave you with quite a long exposure, so it's a good idea to use a cable release to prevent jogging the camera when you press the shutter.

You can also set the camera to self-timer, standing well back during the exposure.

Chapter 7
People and Cars

The majority of photographs taken around the world each year are of people. Family and friends are some of our favorite subjects and they can be captured best in an informal environment so you get a picture of your subject looking happy and relaxed.

However take them out of that comfortable environment and stand them next to a large inanimate object like a car for a photo and you have the recipe for a disaster. An awkward pose, a rigid expression, and a sense of embarrassment all add up to picture that will never make the album.

There are two reasons why it is hard to take good pictures of people with cars. First, people are soft vertical curvy subjects; that is, they stand upright and need to be treated as such when composing your portrait. Cars are hard, angular, horizontal subjects and the two don't go well together naturally. Second, tell anyone to stand in

Connecting your subject with the car is one of the most basic principles of shooting people with cars. By doing so you draw two points of interest into one and draw the focus to the image as a whole and not its component parts. Land speed record holder Andy Green with Thrust 2. 50mm 1/60 second f11.

front of something for a photo and, unless they are an experienced model used to being photographed, they will freeze and assume an unnatural pose.

To get around this, you need to connect your subject with the car to reduce the differences between them and make them feel comfortable in front of your lens. Different techniques work for different situations. Older people, for example, may not want to lie on the ground or drape themselves across the hood, so you'll need to find an appropriate pose for each portrait you shoot.

When photographing tall people, get them to crouch down or lean against the highest part of the car (usually the edge of the windshield) for the shot. Ask them to put a

Try to get your subject in character by asking them how they would like to be photographed. They may have a favorite location, hat, or some other good idea that you should consider. 50mm 1/125 second f11.

Bring your subject into the foreground of your picture. This will focus attention on them and even up their size in relation to the car. Use a pop of fill-in flash 1/2 stop under the aperture to give any shadows on your subject a lift. 35mm 1/15 second f5.6.

hand or an arm on the car, or to sit on the fender or behind the wheel, so that the person and car don't appear to be two separate subjects in one image.

Get your subjects involved in the picture by suggesting something they might wear or hold for the picture. If a driver has just won a race, maybe the winner's wreath could go around his neck or he could hold a checkered flag.

Don't position your subjects so that their shoulders are square to the camera because they won't look relaxed. A good way to avoid this is to ask them to turn their feet horizontal to the camera and get them to swivel from their hips to bring their face back around to the lens. Seek a pose your subject is happy with and that gives you good composition.

While you are setting up the picture, keep talking to them all the time. Although you have plenty to think about during the portrait, they do not, and will only start to worry that they won't look good in the picture.

Be prepared and don't take too long. Check your camera carefully beforehand to make sure you have enough film left, the right lens, and if you need it, your flash gun loaded with fresh batteries. There is nothing worse for the picture than to keep your subject waiting while you take another light reading and fiddle with changing rolls. You'll lose the moment and your subject will just look bored. This is even more important if you get the opportunity to shoot a race driver at a track or bump into a celebrity at a show. Most won't mind if you ask them for a photo, but you will probably only get one chance so make sure that you are completely ready before you ask them.

When composing your picture, it's a good idea is to put your subject in the foreground. This will even up the size of the car in the frame and a pop of fill-in flash set at one stop under your aperture will lift the lighting enough to fill in any shadows on their face.

Also, try using some of the ideas mentioned earlier in the composition section of this book. With the rule of thirds, try not to place your subject in the middle of the frame; move them off to one side looking into the body of the picture. Don't shoot from head height. Find an elevated position out of a window or from a short stepladder,

Use shapes in the foreground to help you compose your shot. Remember the rule of thirds and try to place your subjects in the frame to reflect that visual harmony. 35mm 1/30 second f16.

or a low angle where you look past the car to your subject. With this view it's good idea to use flash, because your subject may be backlit by the sky.

If you want to shoot one person with a group of cars, you might want to use a longer lens to flatten the perspective and draw all the individual parts together. Another good idea is to get some height and place your subject in the foreground with all the cars behind.

If you have a group of people to shoot with one car, stand them behind it and make sure the tallest person is behind the highest part of the car and the shortest is behind the lowest part of the car.

Look around the car to see if it has any outstanding features that catch the eye and include it in the picture but be careful not to let it dominate the image. If it's a convertible, try shooting looking down into the cockpit with your subject on the back seat or behind the wheel.

SHAKE, RATTLE, AND ROLL

Remember to use your tripod at shutter speeds under a 1/30 second with a wide and standard lens and 1/60 second with a telephoto. You can experiment shooting some portraits hand-held with a wide angle in low light and on really slow speeds, such as 1/4 or 1/2 second. Let the flash freeze your subject.

Change your viewpoint so that your subject relates to the camera in a different way. If you do use a wide-angle lens, make sure your subject is in the center to reduce any distortion. 35mm 1/125 second f8.

Choose your lens carefully. A wide lens close up will distort around the edges, so try not to place your subject near the edge of the frame unless you want that effect. A long lens will flatten the image and can look impersonal as though there is no relationship between the subject and the photographer, but may be ideal if you only want to shoot a head-and-shoulders portrait. A standard or a short telephoto lens, such as an 85mm, provides a good balance.

Consider your aperture as well. Many portrait and fashion photographs are taken with a very limited depth of field so the background blurs away into just shapes and colors. It is fine to focus your attention onto the subject, but you may miss the Formula 1 car they are sitting on. A good idea if you want to shoot this way is to include a shape of the car in the foreground or background so you can get some context into the picture.

Black and white is still a great choice for portraits, particularly if you have your own dark room. Placing the subject small in the frame can have as much impact if the image has strong composition. 35mm 1/60 second f5.6.

REVIEW
- **Connect your subject with the car.**
- **Don't shoot from head height.**
- **Use flash to fill any facial shadows.**
- **Keep talking to relax your subject.**
- **Try not to use a wide lens too close.**
- **Don't take too long.**

Chapter 8
Studio Techniques

The whole concept of bringing a car into the studio is so that you can totally control the environment, enhancing the image by removing all distraction and completely focusing on the car. Shot on a 5x4 camera. 360mm 8 seconds f45.

It is rare for the amateur photographer to see inside the mysterious world of the car studio. It is one of the most highly protected areas in the car industry for two reasons: the techniques used, and the new product secrecy that is endemic in the car world.

"Scoop" photographers who can get a photo of a new car to the press before it is launched will earn themselves a fat fee from the magazines who want to know what it looks like. The photos could damage sales of the existing model because some buyers await release of the new one. They can also create a false impression of how the new model will look if the design process is unfinished. Yes, much of the photography for new cars is done in secret—very often on-site in the manufacturer's own studio and away from snooping snappers.

This is a wide view of how the Mercedes on black was shot. The drapes only need to go immediately around the car so that most of the studio can reflect light back onto the car from the walls and the floating ceiling. The silver card is picking up light from the 1K near the camera to reflect into the back wheel.

This is one of the best angles for illustrating a racing car, but you will need a studio with a high roof and safe access above the cove. It's a good idea to put a large polyboard over the car to protect it in case you drop something while setting up. 5x4 camera, 135mm 4 seconds f22.

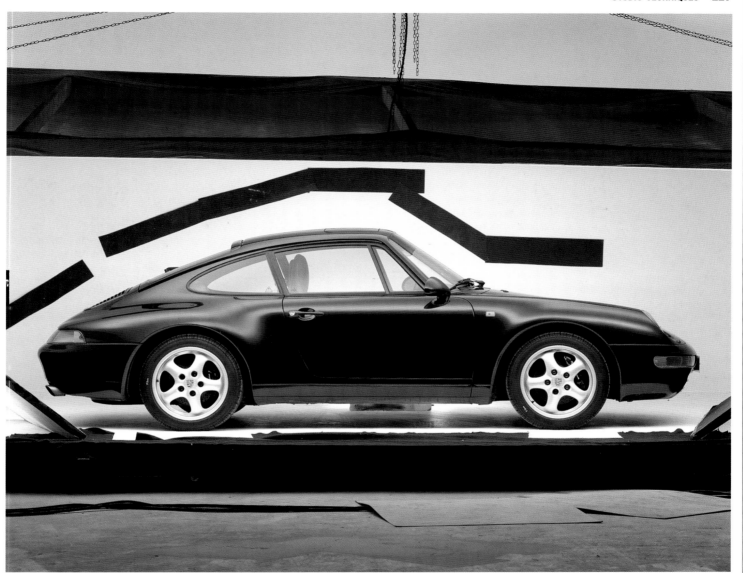

To assist the layout artists to cut out the car for use in a magazine, it helps to give them a solid line along the very edge of where the car meets the studio wall. To do this, get your assistant to stick black tape or card onto the wall above and behind the car so that it reflects a hard edge back into the roofline. You will need to be looking through the camera as the tape goes up to get it in exactly the right position.

The photographers also keep their own techniques to themselves and it is rare for them to allow other photographers into the studio if they are shooting. This is because most work is at the top end of the advertising business, where the fees can be huge, as are the stakes, and photographers can't take any risks of losing the business, or of a rival sneaking a snap and selling it to a magazine as a spoiler.

In recent years, due to competition among the magazines and the fact that studios' prices have come down, editorial photographers have started to shoot cars in the studio. But many have foundered due to the totally different way of working from location photography.

Because there are as many studio techniques as there are locations, we will stick to straightforward salon lighting for this chapter. This is ideal to show off the shape and beauty of the car and can either be left on a plain white background or cutout using your computer and placed on another.

To this end the most effective car studios are either large white or mid-grey spaces where the floor rises up to meet the walls and walls curve in to meet the ceiling. This is called an infinity cove and allows the photographer to reflect light onto the car in a very controlled way by pointing the beams into the walls and ceiling.

Many studios will have a floating ceiling that can be raised or lowered and drawn nearer or further away from the car to bounce light onto it. They also should have a selection of large polystyrene boards about 8x4, some painted black for use in flagging lights, and some left clean white to bounce lights off of.

Although studio flash can be used, particularly if people need to be in the pictures, most car studio photography uses constant focusing tungsten lighting similar to that used in the movie industry. These lights can usually be hired, along with stands, flags, and drapes, from the studio, but you should check that they have everything you need before the day of the shoot in order to save time. Lighting usually comes in 800w, 1K, 2K, and 5K sizes, and will need barn doors on the front and a special high-power cabling and supply. Don't try plugging the large lights in at home because you will probably blow the main fuse.

If you are going to use tungsten lights, make sure you shoot with tungsten-balanced film or use a color correcting filter on the camera to prevent your pictures from coming out orange.

Most studio car photographers will use a monorail camera and large individual sheets of film or high-powered digital backs. This type of camera allows for the focal plane to be shifted, extending the depth of field by moving the lens panel in the same direction as the subject. (They use this equipment only because the image may need to be blown up for giant billboard advertising, and excellent results can be achieved using cameras that use smaller format film.)

SIZE ISN'T EVERYTHING

Match the studio to the car. If you will be shooting a truck you will need a large studio, but if it's a Mini you will want something smaller. If you end up shooting a small car in a large studio, you will waste time and money with extra lighting that you didn't need and may struggle focusing your lights accurately. If you can get the truck into the small studio, you may not have enough room to place your lights, flag them properly, or get back far enough with the camera.

Because you won't be shooting rolls of film, but individual sheets, and given that there is no TTL meter on a large format camera, most photographers will use polaroid film to preview the image. Choose the type that includes a negative and check it for sharpness with an eyepiece.

Due to the long exposures needed—sometimes up to 30 seconds—it is essential to use a cable release to press the shutter and avoid jogging the camera. Use one with a locking mechanism if possible or shoot with the lens in the T position, which opens and closes the shutter each time the release is pressed.

Seen from the other angle set up for a front shot, the floating ceiling has been lowered and rotated to run along the car and reflect more light onto it. Note the large polyboards protecting the camera from any flare.

Opposite: Black cloth or card can be used to reflect back into the car to show off chrome and bodyline. Here, the floating ceiling has been turned so that its back edge creates the line in the windshield when highlighted. 5x4 camera, 300mm 12 seconds f45.

It is essential that your studio car is thoroughly cleaned and the studio is freshly painted before you start your shoot. Any marks on the car or on the floor will leap out at you when you see the photographs, so make sure all is as you want it. If you are shooting an older car, be aware that despite the owner assuring you that his car is in concours condition and in the shape it was when it came out of the factory, under the harsh glare of the studio lights many marks and small dents may be visible.

Start out with the car toward the back of the cove with an equal number of lights half way down on each side and pointing into the side walls. The best set-up to use for general lighting is 2Ks on low floor stands, as they are easier to flag from both the car and the camera. The tires may leave black marks on the floor, so you may need to repaint around the car once you are happy with its position. On the other hand, you may find that the studio will have a set of skates to jack the car onto that won't leave any marks.

You will need an assistant to help you set up the lighting, because you will have to be behind the camera. Make sure your assistants have a good pair of leather gloves to protect their hands because the lights will be very hot. Start out with each light focused to a spot on the side walls and get your assistant to move them individually around the walls and ceiling to see their effect.

If you are shooting a profile, you may need to lower the floating ceiling and draw it in closer to the car. This will weigh down the rear to angle the flat surface toward the car. Remove anything that might be visible from a reflection in the side of the car and flag the lights carefully so that it is as dark as possible around the camera. When you are happy with the position of your lights, flood them to soften the edge of the reflection and move in the barn doors enough so that any light does not spill onto the car. Be careful not to create any shadows that may affect your lighting when moving the barn doors.

A light on the back wall is a must to separate the car from it, but don't make it too bright as you may lose the edge of the roofline. If you do have this problem, try sticking a line of black tape on the back wall so that it reflects back onto the edge of the roof as seen from camera.

If you are shooting a three-quarters view, you might consider reflecting some black drape into the side of the car. This will put a black line down the side of the car that will pick out the shape and create greater contrast in your picture.

To do this, connect two lighting stands with a long pole and hang the black drape over it so that it covers the floor in between the car and the wall. Place your lights on the spot behind it, shining down the length of the wall, so that you create an artificial horizon reflected back onto the car. Be careful not to let the black drapes touch the

Opposite: It is a good idea to check your images on instant film to be certain they are sharp and there are no problems with exposure. Type 55 Polaroid has the added advantage of including a negative that makes it more accurate and, once fixed, creates beautiful fine -rain prints that you can use afterwards 360 mm 8 seconds f32.

tires or cut into the shape around the car. This will cause problems should you want to cut out the car using your computerized imaging software at a later date.

One of the most spectacular shots of a car in the studio is a plan view (overhead shot) taken from dead above the car. It is particularly good for convertibles. For this you will need a studio with a high roof and safe access above the cove. Line up the camera and car very carefully because this shot relies on symmetry for most of its strength. If you are only a bit off to one side it will spoil the effect. Place a large poly-board sheet on the roof of the car while you are setting up so if you do drop anything it won't damage the car. Bring the floating ceiling to maximum height so that you are only shooting through a crack in between it and the studio ceiling; this will maximize the area of ceiling reflected back down onto the car.

Once you are happy with your lighting, pay attention to any unwelcome highlights reflecting back directly from the lights into the car. They usually appear on curved surfaces such as chrome hubcaps or bumper ends and can be tricky to get rid of. Flag them with a card, making sure you can't see the card reflected in the car. If you can't get rid of them, or have any other nasty small reflections, try a little semi-matte dulling spray applied sparingly to the area. Be careful not to overdo it, or you will see the spray and have to remove it and start again.

Also, make sure that you have told the owner what you are going to do. Reassure him that you are not repainting his car, and that the dulling spray will just wipe off with a soft cloth afterward. It's a good habit to flag the camera as well so you won't get any flare entering the lens

REVIEW
- **Choose your studio to suit the car.**
- **Shoot Polaroid to check your exposures.**
- **Use a cable release to avoid camera shake.**
- **Flag the camera and the car from any stray light.**
- **Get an assistant to help out.**
- **Pay great attention to detail.**

Chapter 9
Restoration Photos

Opposite: Photographs taken during a long restoration are not only there as a record of the workmanship and hours that went into rebuilding your pride and joy, they can often be of great assistance when the time comes to put everything back together. 35mm 1/30 second f8.

This is a totally different type of photography from what we have been talking about in this book so far and that's why I decided to put in a special section dedicated to it.

The pictures you want to take during the restoration of a car are there for one thing only: information. They don't need to be arty or express your inner angst. They need to be clear, well lit, and sharp. It's about as close to forensic photography as most of us will want to come.

If you need to reassemble parts in a certain order or have a record of what a section of body looks like before you take the blowtorch to it, take a few pictures to illustrate the scene. For close-ups you'll need a 35mm SLR with a macro lens and, ideally, a tripod. Since the color of the light doesn't usually matter, you can shoot long exposures to make sure you have a large enough depth of field to get everything sharp. Don't just take one image if it's an important stage you are recording; take a few, maybe from different angles.

Use a hand-held flash to cast light into dark corners and particularly if you are shooting the underside of the car, which will probably be black and grimy and will absorb a lot of light. If you have a manual flash gun try bracketing the exposure by shooting a couple of frames with the power turned up and one or two with it turned down. This way you'll be sure to get the shot.

If you need to have hands in the frame of an engine bay and pointing at a certain component, rub in a little dirty oil, or wear protective gloves to darken light-colored skin. Pale skin may affect the flash and make it hard to see what you are trying to show, due to the highlight bouncing off your hand.

The next most important thing to do when you see your photos is to label them. This is vital for remembering what it is you shot, which way up it went, and when you shot it.

It is best to use print film or digital media for this as they have better exposure latitude and hence a greater margin for error. Compact cameras are ideal; they automatically put in just the right amount of flash—but don't get too close, as they will usually only focus beyond three feet. 50mm 1/15 second f11.

Many restorers will put all the photos in an album after they have finished with the restoration to remind themselves and their family never to undertake another!

REVIEW

■ *Use your photographs to record information.*

■ *Use a tripod and a large depth of field.*

■ *Label your images carefully as soon as you can.*

MODELS

Photographing model cars can be just as tricky as shooting the real thing. You have to remember all the rules for exposure and reflection and contend with the problems of depth of focus that go along with shooting something small.

The quickest and simplest way to get good results is to build a studio in miniature and take it outside on a cloudy day. All you will need is a piece of white or grey card and a

table to work on. You will also need a close focusing lens, or macro lens, for your camera. Most compact cameras won't have one of these, so you will need a 35mm SLR or medium format.

Mount the camera on a medium-sized tripod and position the model on the card in front of it. The rule here is to be sure you have a small enough aperture to extend the depth of focus over the whole subject. This is important due to the tiny depth of field increments when using a macro lens—with the aperture wide open these may be as little as a few millimeters.

Use your depth of field preview button, which is usually located on the body near the lens mount, or on the lens, to check that the model is sharp from nose to tail. The

The smaller the model, the more depth of field and smaller aperture you will need. It's useful when shooting particularly small or large models to use the most common sized 1:43 scale as a guide. 50mm 1/8 second f32.

For best results, build a mini-studio outside on a cloudy day. If it's sunny you can use a sheet of diffusing paper to soften the light source. Use a tripod as you may need long exposures to get your maximum depth of field.
50mm 1/2 second f32.

smaller the model, the greater the problem with depth of field. So with a model at 1:43, about two and a half inches long, you will need to shoot using the smallest aperture on your lens. If this is still not enough and the model appears unsharp in places, focus one-third into the model and check your depth of field again.

After you are content that all will be sharp, think about how the model is lit. The best and most even light is supplied by a bright cloudy sky. Don't shoot in shadow on a sunny day as this may make your pictures look very blue. If you want to shoot in the sun, stretch a piece of tracing or baking paper over the top of your studio, which will diffuse the light nicely. Use pieces of black or white card to reflect light into the side of the car or to flag out any nasty reflections.

Alternatively, you may be able to shoot on a small diorama. This is a scene in miniature to set the car in and could be anything from a racetrack to a town square. You can make them yourself or buy a kit from a model store. If your local car modeler doesn't have any, try the railway model store as they often have a better selection.

If you are unable to shoot outside you can set up your studio inside, but you will need some lights. The easiest way is to use a couple of angle poise lights shining through the tracing or baking paper.

If you are shooting on print film, you will need a blue color correction filter on the front of the camera or your pictures will turn out orange. If you are shooting on transparency, remember to ask for tungsten film. Digital will be fine, but you may need to press the white balance button before you start out.

Set your lights at 45 degrees and pointing down to the tabletop exactly the same distance from the model. If they are unequal distances, you will start to get shadows appearing around the model. You may need exposures of one or two seconds so make sure your tripod is steady and use a cable release or the self-timer to avoid any camera shake.

REVIEW

- ■ *Put the camera on a tripod when using a macro lens.*
- ■ *Think carefully about your background.*
- ■ *Use the smallest aperture to gain the greatest depth of field.*
- ■ *Shoot outside on a cloudy day.*

An alternative to the mini-studio idea is to build a diorama or shoot your cars on a Scalectrix or similar racetrack. This is lit too harshly by flash and would have been better shot outside if there had been an opportunity. 35mm 1/30 second f8.

Chapter 10
Shooting a Magazine Feature

Around the world today there are hundreds of magazines that specialize in cars. Someone has got to shoot all those pictures and it could be you. Throughout this book I have been demonstrating that with a good eye, plenty of patience, and practice, there is no myth or mystery about shooting great car images.

In this chapter we will go through just what it takes to get a set of your photographs into the pages of your favorite car magazine.

GETTING THE JOB

If there are hundreds of car magazines in the world, there are thousands of photographers who want to shoot for them. So how do you get your first commission? It's a bit of a catch-22 situation. You need to show an art editor a set of fantastic pictures, preferably from another publication. If you have never been published you need to show them a portfolio of work that demonstrates you can take the kind of pictures that they feature in their magazine.

This should be a well-presented set of 12-20 images on medium format transparency or

prints, window mounted into card. There is no point rattling through 50 or a 100 of your unedited pictures on the art editor's desk, as they will be short of time and unimpressed with your organization.

Ask their advice. Which pictures do they like and not like? Don't be too sensitive; use this information to hone your choice of images, dropping the unpopular ones and replacing them with new work.

THE BRIEF

If you haven't worked for a magazine before they may give you a brief to tell you what the feature is about and what they are looking for in your pictures. The art director or art editor may also come on the shoot with you. The relationship you have with them is very important—you are a team, with each of you fulfilling your roles to a common goal. So try to accommodate their ideas even if you have different

A potential lead shot is often a landscape version of your cover image. This needs to be a strong static shot with space to drop text if necessary. Keep the background as simple as possible. 300mm 1/15 second f16. **Opposite:** If you have been asked to come up with a cover image, it's a good idea to shoot a portrait version of your lead image. Leave enough space around the car to allow the layout artist to drop in the magazine name and other cover wording. If you are shooting with sky at the top of the frame, reduce the contrast by using a graduated neutral density filter to balance the brightness of the picture. 200mm 1/8 second f16

Top: Make time for some shots you haven't tried before and experiment. Here, the lightweight camera is mounted onto a suction device on the body facing the wheel, with a remote trigger attached to the hot shoe. **Above:** The camera is fired by remote control to prevent jogging the exposure and shot at one or two miles per hour with the engine switched off to avoid any vibration. 20-35mm zoom 4 seconds f22.

ones on how you think the shoot should go. This can be more difficult than you think, as no two people will see the same thing.

If you are confident and build up their trust, they are more likely to leave you alone to get on with the job. A good way to build confidence is to get to know the magazine. Study back issues to see how they do things, what their editorial attitude is, and how they lay out their pictures. Do they place images in boxes or do they bleed right to the edge of the page? Get the art editor to go through an issue with you and say what he does or doesn't like. Suggest some style options for your shoot. Has he thought of shooting it in black and white, cross-processing the film, or doing the whole thing naked in the local swimming pool?! Any ideas you have, whether they are accepted or not, will be listened to, because magazines are always looking for something new, different, and original.

Find out how many pages the feature will be and if they are expecting you to come up with a cover image. This will be very important when it comes to the shoot because you will need to know how many pictures to take and allow more time for a specialized cover shot.

Think about the feature from the art editor's point of view. He will need a lead static shot, preferably on medium format so it can be used as an opener across a double-page spread, a lead action shot that could also be used as an opener shot on 35mm, and a good selection of other action and details shots to illustrate the feature with. The more choice you can offer, the better.

THE SHOOT

There are a number of key elements that go in to making a successful shoot.

The choice of location is probably the most important. Discuss with the art director what sort of location he thinks would work for the feature car and suggest some options. Try to choose a place that allows you to cover as many of your main images as possible in and around the same location. You may have to drive a long way to get the right place, but when you do it will save time and will make a huge difference in the final photographs.

The weather is something you can't do much about. But you can listen to forecasts and look at the weather satellite information on the Internet to plan which day of the week looks more favorable. On the appointed day you'll have to go with whatever weather you get, so it's better to know than not know. There are also weather call centers that will fairly accurately predict how the weather is changing throughout the day and can give some hope if you're stuck in a downpour.

You and Your Equipment

Be confident but aware of the pitfalls. Take your time and remember all the lessons you have learned along the way. Check your cameras and lenses the day before to make sure they are all working properly and that you have new batteries installed with spares in your bag with the film. If you don't have the right long lenses or need something special, hire it from a pro camera store. If it's something really unusual you may even get the magazine to pay for it.

Always have a back-up camera. If you are shooting your main images on medium format, back them up on 35mm. This not only gives you an element of insurance if something goes wrong with your camera, but also a slightly different format for the art editor to choose from when the photos are processed. It also adds little to the cost.

The Car

As I've mentioned, you have a better chance of getting a fantastic shot of a brand-new Ferrari on the quay in Monte Carlo at sunrise than you do shooting a beat-up Ford sedan on a side street in East L.A. But trying to turn your liabilities into assets is one of the best rules to learn. Maybe you could shoot the sedan on black and white high-speed grainy film and go for the city grunge feel or cross process and go for weird colors and contrasts.

Make sure the car looks its best before you shoot. Although magazines can remove antennae and clean up dirty marks on the body on computer, they can't close windows or straighten tires. So double-check before you press the shutter and if you have any doubts, don't shoot. Sort out potential problems immediately, because you will kick yourself if you see the problem in your final image.

It is very important that you meter carefully when shooting interiors. A black leather interior like this will absorb at least a whole stop when metered though your TTL meter, so it is essential that you take a secondary reading or risk over-exposing your film.

EXTRA DRIVER

On the day of the shoot try to take along an extra driver. Remember, if you are going to do car-to-car tracking shots you will need two cars and two experienced drivers. Think about the type of car you are going to bring and make sure it is suitable to be used as a camera car. Don't go for under-powered sedans with no suspension. Do go for convertibles and hot hatchbacks.

An alternative to a static lead is a dynamic action shot. Tracking and cornering work best from as low an angle as you can go. This winter shoot works well with the silver color of the Mercedes SLK. 300mm 1/500 second f4.

On Location

When you arrive at your location spend some time looking around for the angle you want for the lead or header shot. Next to the cover shot, this is the most important picture you will shoot that day, so take your time choosing the right spot to place the car. If you see somewhere better later on, shoot that too—but it's preferable to get it right the first time.

You may spend a long time adjusting the position of the camera or the car or waiting for the light to move, but that's okay. This is the shot that will make the reader stop and look at your pictures when they appear in the pages of the magazine, so take your time. If you are hanging around waiting for the light, think about whether you can shoot any details while you are waiting without moving the car.

Once you are happy with the image, shoot it and a few alternatives from near the same angle. The more choice you can give the art editors, the more likely they are to use you again.

When shooting head or taillights as details, turn them on. You can leave flashers going and brake lights on for long exposures but only need to flash headlights for 1/2 second during the exposure to avoid risk of flare into the lens.

Panning shots from above show another dimension to the car and look great. Be aware that if the car is traveling uphill or downhill, you will need to adjust your focus as it advances or use autofocus. 180mm 1/60 second f4.5.

A landscape shot is favored by art editors as a good establishing image or another option for a lead, so it's always worth doing. Use the road to guide the eye into the image. 300mm 1/500 second f5.6.

Many car magazines now only use dynamic action shots on their covers to grab the buyer's attention at the news stand. A cornering or a tracking shot has the highest impact for a cover action image. If the light conditions and the roads allow, do both. Try to get your car facing to the right in the frame to lead the eye onto the open side of the magazine.

For a cornering shot, get as low as you can with your long lens, from 180-300mm is ideal, and just watch the car around the corner for the first few runs. You are look-ing for the point when the car is at the apex of the bend and at its maximum limit of suspension and lean. Many high-performance cars will only reach this at very high speeds, so don't be concerned if the car's not dragging its wheel arches through the bend; concentrate on getting the best shot you can.

Remember all the safety rules, particularly if you are shooting on a public road with other traffic.

REVIEW

- **Stick to the brief.**
- **Get to know the magazine.**
- **If you have time, check out the location before the shoot.**
- **Check weather forecasts on the Internet.**
- **Be confident and keep calm if anything goes wrong.**
- **Set up a watcher to warn of other cars coming.**
- **Try to give the art editor as many options as possible.**
- **Don't ask your drivers to drive beyond their ability.**
- **Make sure your work is well presented.**

If there is no shade around on a bright sunny day, create some to shoot your details. Engines will offer far too much contrast if shot in full sun, with a loss of detail in the shadows and the highlights. Use whatever you can to gain a bit of height and a different angle of view.

Chapter 11
Photographic Archiving

DIGITAL

Storage of your photographs has just become a whole lot easier with the greater accessibility and capacity of digital archiving. This can be set up with basic home computer equipment and doesn't have to cost a fortune.

What You Need

You'll need a home computer with a basic photographic software package. These are usually included in the application already installed on the computer at purchase or when you buy a scanner. If not, contact your area computer store to get a simple package such as:

- a flatbed scanner preferably with a transparency hood. This will be good for prints up to A4 and larger transparencies.
- A 35mm film scanner. This will be used for your 35mm transparencies and negatives.

- A CD burner. This will cut your own CDs to record your images onto 700 MB discs.

For prints up to A4, simply use your flatbed scanner. Be sure to carefully clean the glass to remove any dust or fingerprints. Set the file size to around 8x12 inches at 300dpi and save it as a TIFF file. This is the best type of file for your archive, as the images can't degrade at all, but it does take up a lot of space. This will give you a file size of about 25 megabytes (MB) and is of good enough quality to reproduce in a magazine.

You can compress your images by using a JPEG format, which allows you reduce the size of the file without much loss of quality. This is a good idea if you have a lot of photos and want to burn them onto a CD to archive them. You will be able to store considerably more images onto the disc.

For instance, that 25MB file will go right down to 1MB scaled to 11x14inches at 72dpi saved as a JPEG file at 6/10th quality. This will make it easy to send by email and with a 56K modem should only take a few seconds. It should fill the screen of your recipient but they won't be able to enlarge it anymore or print out a decent copy.

If you just want to store at a lower resolution or for sending by email, use a larger size and save at 72dpi. You may also be able to save your Web-sized images as GIF files, which are specially designed for the Internet.

If you want to save your 35mm transparencies digitally you'll need a film scanner to get any quality. You can use the transparency hood on a flatbed scanner, but they are not really designed for small images and the quality is poor. You may find that this will work okay if you only want to scan for the Web or to send by email, but for most other uses it's no good. Medium or large format transparencies do work well, however, so don't throw out the hood as a useless accessory just in case you upgrade your photographic gear.

The film scanner works in two ways. It is possible to insert a single mounted transparency, which is then sucked into the slot on the front to be scanned. If you choose this method, make sure that you use a rigid plastic slide mount because the film can distort in the scanner and you'll end up with a wobbly scanned image. It is better to use the carrier that holds a strip of six transparencies or negatives. This will still only scan a single image at a time, but secures the film better and consequently gives better results.

Save your files as with the flatbed images mentioned earlier. You can reverse negatives to positives by using the imaging software—or save them as negatives.

When you have enough images to fill a CD, 650MB, burn them, remembering to label the files and the outside of the box so you can find them again. Remember, there are two types of recordable CD so make sure you get the right one. CD-R is the

Opposite: Archiving your images has been made a whole lot easier by digital technology. Using your home computer, it's now easy to scan your images, retouch them, and burn them onto a CD in a matter of minutes.

Despite many technology companies ringing the death knell of film, it's going to be around for quite a while yet. Storage can get bulky so only file your best images and consign your "overs" to the bin or a box in the attic.

Opposite: It's fine to take pictures of famous drivers and it's okay to sell them to a magazine to be used in editorial, but you can't use that same image for any advertising or promotion without their express permission.

cheapest type but whatever you write onto the CD is permanent and once the disc is full you can't swap images or erase. CD-RW is more expensive but allows you to remove images and reuse the disc for something else.

It's a good idea to theme your CDs. So you may have "Racing Images" on one, "Car Shows" on another, etc.

REVIEW

TIFF Save your images as a TIFF file if you want top-quality for printing, reproduction in a magazine, and long-term archiving.

JPEG Save as a JPEG for compressing large numbers of images onto CDs with a varying loss of quality. okay for printing at the higher end and for the Web at the lower end.

GIF Save as a GIF only for the Web.

NON-DIGITAL

Over the years that photography has been around most people have just stored their photos in an album. There are many different types and some are better than others for storing your pictures long-term and keeping them safe.

The old-fashioned type where you attach the photo at the corners with a flyleaf of thin paper covering each page are the best, but they are expensive and can be difficult to find. The advantage here is that you can mount any size of print into the album and are not just stuck with 4x6 inches. It's also good to look for ones that are made from acid-free paper, as this will ensure your pictures won't discolor over the years.

Steer away from the albums with a sticky surface that holds your pictures and a clear plastic sheet on top. As they get older, the glue fails and all your photos will end up in a heap on the floor next time you lift the album out of the bookshelf. The glue can also have chemicals in it that will discolor the print and the plastic sheet can stick hard to the front of the print. If this happens, don't try to tear it away because you may damage the print. Soak the whole page in some warm water and tease the print away from the page with a blunt instrument. If you don't feel confident, take it to your nearest photo lab and ask them to do it.

A cheaper and better option are the flip albums that have an individual slip for each image. There's no glue involved and the prints are quick and easy to insert. However, they usually only come in the 4x6 inches format.

Transparencies and negatives can be stored in strips of five or six to a page and kept in a lever-arch file. There are a number of photographic accessory companies that make many different shapes and sizes specifically for this purpose. They also make pages to hold single-mounted slides and hanging files to use in a filing cabinet.

Don't forget to label your files and the individual pages so your pictures are easy to find when you need them.

Legal Issues

There are few legal issues that arise photographing cars, as long as you stay on the right side of the traffic cops when shooting on the open roads.

If you include people in your photographs and intend to publish or use them in any way commercially, you should gain their permission and ask them to sign a model release form. This is a simple legal document that means they can't come back to you when they see their image on a billboard and sue. They are available preprinted from good pro-stores or you can draft your own, but get a friendly lawyer to run through it to make sure you haven't missed anything.

Most professional photographers also have public liability insurance that covers them in case of an accident in a public place. More often than not you will not be allowed to shoot on some sites without it. You can usually

If you want to use locations such as airports and race tracks you will need to prove you have public liability insurance. This is not expensive and you can usually add it to your camera equipment policy.

get this as part of your camera cover and should have at least $5 million for it to be worthwhile.

If you decide to snap a scoop shot of a secret car testing that you come across, be careful; in some countries this is considered industrial espionage and you could end up in jail.

Many of the techniques described in this book sound dangerous but with the right precautions are very safe. Always obey speed limits and traffic signs; but if you do get stopped by a curious law officer, be polite and carefully explain what you are doing.

Best of luck on your future developments.

Index

Other MBI Publishing Company titles by the author:

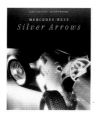

Mercedes-Benz Silver Arrows
ISBN 3-7688-1377-0

Mercedes-Benz
0-7603-0949-3

Ferrari 330/P4
ISBN 0-7603-1081-5

Corvette: Fifty Years
ISBN 0-7603-1180-3

Hemi: The Ultimate American V-8
ISBN 0-7603-1103-X

American Drag Racing
ISBN 0-7603-0871-3

The American Auto Factory
ISBN 0-7603-1059-9

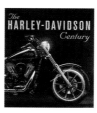

The Harley-Davidson Century
ISBN 0-7603-1155-2

Snakes in the Cockpit: Images of Military Aviation Disasters
ISBN 0-7603-1250-8

Find us on the Internet at www.motorbooks.com   1-800-826-6600